Hacking Essentials
Study Guide and Workbook
Volume 3

Created by: Pete Herzog
Marta Barceló Jordan
Bob Monroe

HACKING IS LEARNING
www.hackerhighschool.org

Table of Contents

WARNING

Hacking is a methodology for learning and as with any learning tool there are dangers. Some lessons, if abused, may result in injury. Some additional dangers may also exist where there is not enough research on possible effects of emanations from particular technologies. Students using these lessons should be supervised yet encouraged to learn, try, and do. However the authors or ISECOM cannot accept responsibility for how any information herein is abused.

ISECOM

Introduction to this Hacking Essentials Study Guide

There are hundreds of books written on networking and each one stands on its own merits. This book was not written to compete with any of those other works. This book was written to speed up the learning process and cut through some of the fluff. Don't bother to read our book if you want to know the names of people who wrote a certain protocol or dates when specific networking milestones occurred. If you want to know which university designed a certain networking function or which company patented a widget, than you picked up the wrong book.

We wrote this manual for speed of learning and ease of information retention.

We are not teaching you to be cracker, rather we are teaching you to work on contemporary and future systems. If you want to be a mechanic, you have to learn how to dissemble an engine. To be a successful network security professional, you need to know the inner workings of your digital world. This world includes portable devices (BYOD), servers, network protocols, hardware, software, security frameworks, principles of trust, virtual machines and dozens of other items.

Flipping through the pages you will notice that this book is not your typical technical guide. We designed everything to keep the reader engaged; to keep you interested. You will find segments like **Feed Your Head**, which are focused on deeper aspects of a topic. There are exercises that aren't just multiple choice questions but require you to actually think through a problem or research to find them. This is not a Dummies guide. This is a Hackers guide; old school hacker style.

The lessons from HackerHighschool.org which this manual follows and expands on have been an enormous task on behalf of the nonprofit Institute for Security and Open Methodologies (ISECOM.org).

Our guiding philosophy is to encourage all people across the world to embrace technology for its uses but not to harm others. Information should be free to the extent that it doesn't infringe on personal privacy or global peace.

Introduction by Pete Herzog

Whatever you may have heard about hackers, the truth is they do something really, really well: discover. Hackers are motivated, resourceful, and creative. They get deeply into how things work, to the point that they know how to take control of them and change them into something else. This lets them re-think even big ideas because they can really dig to the bottom of how things function. Furthermore, they aren't afraid to make the same mistake twice just out of a kind of scientific curiosity, to see if that mistake always has the same results. That's why hackers don't see failure as a mistake or a waste of time because every failure means something and something new to be learned. And these are all traits any society needs in order to make progress.

> Many people who have been called hackers, especially by the media, or who have gotten in trouble for "hacking" were not, in fact, hackers.

A hacker is a type of hands-on, experimenting scientist, although perhaps sometimes the term "mad scientist" fits better since unlike professional scientists, they dive right in following a feeling rather than a formal hypothesis. That's not necessarily a bad thing. Many interesting things have been designed or invented by people who didn't follow standard conventions of what was known or believed to be true at the time.

The mathematician, *Georg Cantor*, proposed new ideas about infinity and set theory that caused outrage amongst many fellow mathematicians to the point that one called his ideas a "grave disease" infecting mathematics.

Nikola Tesla is another person considered a "mad scientist" in his day, but he knew more about how electricity behaved than anyone else. He designed possibly the first brushless motor that ran on AC electricity but is mostly known for the Tesla effect and the Tesla coil.

Then there was *Ignaz Philipp Semmelweis* who figured out that doctors need to wash their hands between treating patients to keep diseases from spreading. He wondered if the diseases following him around between patients were his fault, so he decided to try washing hands between his patient visits and sure enough, the transmissions disappeared. His ideas went against both the scientific conventions of what was known at the time about germs (nothing) as well as the convenience of the doctors who felt it was too much hassle to keep washing their hands.

What you may think you know about hackers is that they can break into other computers and take over other people's accounts. They can read your email without you knowing. They can look through your web cam without your permission and can see you and hear you in the supposed privacy of your own home. That's not untrue.

Some hackers see network security as just another challenge, so they tinker with ways to trick or fool the system, but really what they're trying to do is out-think the network installers or designers. They discover as much about the network as they can, where it gets its instructions, the rules it uses, and how it interacts with operating systems, the other systems around it, the users who have access to it and the administrators who manage it. Then they use that to try different ways of getting what they want. This kind of hacking can be greatly beneficial to the world for understanding how to be safer and for building even better technology.

Unfortunately though, sometimes the hacking is done by criminals and what they want is illegal, invasive, and destructive. And those are usually the only hackers you read about in the news.

A hacker is not someone who posts to someone's account when they leave some social media page open or **shoulder-surfs** passwords and then logs into their account later. That's not hacking. A hacker also is not someone who downloads a **script kiddie** tool to break into someone's email. Those aren't hackers; those are just thieves and vandals.

Hacking is research. Have you ever tried something again and again in different ways to get it to do what you wanted? Have you ever opened up a machine or a device to see how it works, research what the components are, and then make adjustments to see what now worked differently? That's hacking. You are hacking whenever you deeply examine how something really works in order to creatively manipulate it into doing what you want.

It just so happens that the way the Internet is designed and the huge number of different applications, systems, devices, and processes it has makes it the most common place to find hackers. You could say it was built by hackers so it's the best playground for hackers. But it's not the only place. You can find great hackers in almost every field and industry and they all have one thing in common: they spend time learning how things work, so they can make them work in a new way. They didn't look at something as the original designers did, but instead saw bigger or better potential for it and hacked it to be something new.

> Don't think you can just be a great hacker. Only by doing great hacks with great humility can you be great.

Hacking itself is not illegal. At least not any more than throwing a rock is illegal. It all comes down to intent. If you throw a rock and your intent is to injure someone, that's a crime. If your intent is not to hurt someone, but someone does get hurt, that may not be a crime, but you are responsible for your actions and will have to pay restitution. An ISECOM project called the **Hacker Profiling Project** found that the most damage from hacking comes from young, inexperienced hackers damaging other people's property by accident. That's like throwing rocks in the street just for fun but denting cars and smashing windows in the process. Maybe the damage is unintentional, but you can expect to be held responsible and pay for it. So do be careful when hacking around other people's property. Stick to hacking your own stuff.

It may be illegal to hack something you bought and own. There are hackers who have been punished for hacking their own devices and computers. There are hackers who hacked programs, music and movies they bought – and were prosecuted for it. In particular, you may not be allowed legally to hack software that you've purchased, even if it's just to check for yourself that it's secure enough to run on your own computer. This is because many of the things that you purchase may come with a contract or **End User License Agreement (EULA)** that says you can't. And you agree to it when you open or install the product, even if you can't read it or even know about it until after you've opened or installed the product. Keep this in mind when you are practicing your hacking skills on the things you purchased in the privacy of your own home.

Being a Hacker

Why Be a Hacker?

Consider how scientists mapped the human genome: they used a method developed for decoding passwords. Passwords are usually stored in an encrypted form, so they're hard to steal. Hierarchical shotgun **brute-forcing** is a method of decrypting passwords by **cracking** their encrypted form. It breaks down the encrypted **hash** of the password, solves a few characters at a time, then stitches it all back together. Genome researchers adapted the same technique to map the entire 3.3 billion base pairs of the human genome.

Hacking has shown up in kitchens as chefs use liquid nitrogen as the cooling agent to make perfect ice cream or when they hack food to make tomato fries with potato sauce as the ketchup or just need to make something they don't have the right equipment for....

Chemists have been hacking elements and compounds for centuries. By nature molecules are finicky when it comes to how they behave in different environments (hot weather, cold weather, on mountains, or deep beneath the ocean), so chemists need to deeply understand the properties of the chemicals they have, so they can try to hack together the one they need. Nowhere is this more evident than in the invention of new pharmaceuticals, where hundreds of plants in a region are studied for their chemical properties from roots to fruits, and extracted and combined with others to make new medicines. Then they try again and again, sometimes for years, to get the combinations right and make it do what they want it to do.

Hacking is used in business to understand a market or the buying behavior of certain types of consumers. They research deeply into the forces that drive the area of business they're concerned with, and then they try to change or influence it to make it do what they want. Sometimes they're hacking the product, and sometimes they're hacking you (with advertising and **priming**, something you'll work with in the Social Engineering lesson).

Hacking has also become an increasingly critical part of warfare. Highly skilled soldiers are resourceful and creative in accomplishing their goals, which is exactly what hackers are. Code breakers, intelligence analysts and field officers use what are basically hacking skills to figure out what the enemy has, what they are doing, and how to take advantage of any weaknesses in their equipment. As more nations rely on computers and networks, the use of hacking in cyber attacks and defense has become a valuable part of a nation's armed forces and intelligence operations. National and international security agencies are even going to hacker conventions to recruit hackers!

> The real reason to be a hacker is because it's really powerful. You can do some very cool things when you have strong hacking skills. Any deep knowledge gives you great power. If you know how something works to the point that you can take control of it, you have serious power in your hands. Most of all, you have the power to protect yourself and those you care about.

More and more of people's lives are online as relationships form, people find jobs, and money is made on the Internet. Information can be valuable – or threatening – and hackers can protect themselves better than anyone else. They can research what's happening to their data. They can make sure to reveal only what they want and just generally keep themselves safer and more private. That's a huge competitive advantage in school, at work, and in life, because the smallest negative perception will eventually be used against you. Count on it.

Feed Your Head: Handles

What's a handle all about?

From the earliest days, hackers had handles. A handle is a made up name that a hacker goes by. This was mostly for fun because hackers in the early days were mostly kids. But later, this game of "playing someone else" became a tool that hackers could use to protect themselves by allowing them to be anonymous.

Early on, hackers chose names like "Erik Bloodaxe," "Mentor" and "Captain Crunch." Some hackers played on the spelling of words like Phiber Optik. Those are the names of some of the most notable, and each is now known publicly.

But hacker handles were meant to be like a super hero's secret identity. No one, or only close trusted friends should know the handle you use online. Why the need for this secrecy? Because sometimes, people don't understand how hackers help, and who we are.

For example, in the past many students who happened to be hackers discovered vulnerabilities in the very networks that they used everyday at school. Wanting to be helpful they reported these findings to school administration. Sometimes the administration was grateful for the information, and maybe even for help with fixing the flaw. But there are several cases when the student was expelled, or even prosecuted by the school system. That reaction comes from ignorance, but it's something that we have to understand and deal with.

Handles also promote free speech. As hackers, we need to say what's true to a world that sometimes doesn't want to hear it. It's a sad fact that some people that hold positions of authority may try to put pressure on a person to bend the truth or hide it when it doesn't agree with their personal views.

The utility of a hacker handle is that it allows us to be ourselves, without the worry of retribution from a well-meaning, but misunderstanding society.

So how does one get started with choosing a handle and establishing an online identity? Well, first things first. Choose a handle that means something to you, and try to make it unique. For example, "Batman" is not very unique, and means something to lots of people. But if you like Windows batch scripts, then BAT.mn is a step closer.

Many handles incorporate parts of **leet speak**. An example is the name used by the group **l0pht**. They chose that name for their group because they met in a rented loft. So you could decide to incorporate that into your chosen handle. If you've become pretty good at playing with Linux's iptables (a host based firewall) you might choose "fyr3w@ll". Just remember that whatever you use, you'll have to type it over and over, so don't go too overboard.

Once you have your handle all picked out, it's time to start establishing your online identity. The first step is the easiest. Go to one of the online providers of free email accounts and see if you can create an account with your new handle. You may find that someone else is using it already. If you do, you can tweak it to be different, change the handle altogether, or simply try the same handle with a different email service.

Once you have your email account established, you need to think about the forums, IRC channels and mailing lists that you want to subscribe to. Forums are a good way for you to establish your new handle. When you are new and inexperienced, you can get help from more seasoned hackers by posting questions to a forum. As you get more experience yourself, you can help others by answering posts that you have experience with. A word of caution here: always research thoroughly before posting questions. If you ask a question that has an obvious answer, you may get terse responses. Always try to be gracious if someone is rude. No one likes a **flame war**.

You can now hang out in IRC, or sign in to instant messaging clients with your new handle.

You can also start a blog, or web page, listing your new handle as the author/administrator. But remember that this will mean a commitment on your part to keep the content updated; so think hard before you commit to something that could be time consuming.

Having established your online secret identity, or handle, you should enjoy keeping it a secret. Don't ever mention yourself, or anyone that you know in your posts, comments or messages. It's easy to keep things anonymous in most cases. If you do accidentally discover that misconfigured webpage, server or computer, then you can send an email from your handle's account, and not worry about the fact that the person that owns it is your principal, club leader, or dad.

You may find, as many hackers do, that as you get older and respected in computer security circles, that you don't need your handle anymore. That you can use your real name and be taken seriously. If you work hard, become proficient and well regarded then you don't need to hide behind anonymity to be taken seriously any longer. And that day can be just as liberating as it was the day that you chose your handle.

-Dzen Hacks

Exercise

1.1 You may or may not choose to use a hacker handle, but you should think about it. As Dzen notes above, you may have a legitimate reason to maintain an alternate identity. So what would your handle be?

How about something dark and mysterious: Phantom Blade or Lightning Fury or Dark Summoner? Can you really live up to this persona? Do you even want to?

Maybe something light and non-threatening? Sk8ter? PonyGirl? Would you be worried about being taken seriously?

Okay, maybe a friendly name like FluffyBunny? Unfortunately, you might be giving the wrong impression about your interests.

The ideal handle is one that never gives you away, but says something about your interests and personality.

Choose a handle for yourself. Design it. Make it yours.

How to Hack

Telling you how to hack is like explaining to you how to do a backward flip on a balance beam: no matter how detailed the explanation is you won't be able to do it on your own the first time. You need to develop the skills, feeling, and intuition through practice or else you'll fall flat on your face. But there are some things we can tell you to help you along and encourage you to keep practicing.

First, you should know some little secrets about how hacking actually works. We're going to take these from the **OSSTMM** (www.osstmm.org). Hackers sound it out and pronounce it "aw-stem." The OSSTMM is the **Open Source Security Testing Methodology Manual**, and while it may read like DVD player setup instructions, it's the main document that many hacking professionals use to plan and execute their attacks and defenses. Deep in that manual are some real gems that will open your eyes.

Two Ways to Get What You Want

For example, you should know that there are really only two ways to take anything: you take it or you have someone else take it and give it to you. That means all the taking in the world requires **interactions** between the person and the thing. Obvious, right? But think about it. That means that all protection mechanisms have to try to stop someone from interacting with the thing they are protecting. Unless you lock everything in a huge safe, you can't stop all interaction. Stores need to put stuff on shelves that shoppers can touch. Businesses need to send information through email clients that attach to mail servers and send messages to other mail servers.

All of these are interactions. Some of these interactions are between people and things that are familiar with each other, so we call those interactions **Trusts**. When the interactions happen between unknown people or systems we call these interactions **Accesses**. You can either use an access to take what you want yourself, or you can trick someone who has a trust with the target to take what you want for you and give it to you. If you think about that for a moment, it means that security means protecting something from both those it doesn't know and those it knows and trusts.

Exercises

1.2   What kind of interaction is using a search engine? Think carefully: is anyone giving Access? Is anyone giving Trust?

1.3   Give a simple example of using Access and Trust to take a bicycle locked to a bike rack.

1.4   Give a simple example of how you can use Access and Trust to log into another person's web-mail account.

Hack everything but harm none.

Feed Your Head: Espionage

When hacking is used against a foreign government to commit criminal acts of breaking and entering, trespassing, theft, and destruction to get the edge in political or military information it's called **espionage**. But when the hacking is done from a foreign business against another business in a different country to get an edge in business, it's called **economic espionage**.

When hacking is used to get private and personal information on individual people to embarrass them publicly it's called **DoXing**. If public information is dug out to target a person or company for an attack, but no criminal acts are made to get the information, it's referred to as **document grinding** or **OSInt (Open Source Intelligence)**.

When hacking is used to understand a company network, systems, applications, and devices as the target of an attack without actually intruding or trespassing into the systems it's known as **network surveying**.

When hacking is used to deeply understand a competitor without breaking any laws (although what they do may be considered just plain mean or rude) it's called **competitive intelligence**.

You're probably dying to hear now what kind of mean and rude things they do that are still legal. Consider the example of inflicting stress and worry on someone to get information from them. As long as you don't kill them, telling them lies is still legal (although there are laws against causing panic in public places like yelling "Fire!" in a crowded movie theater when there is none).

Say the hacker wants to know where a company is planning to set up their new factory. They use document grinding to find out which people are in the position to make that decision. Then the hacker calls their offices to find out which cities they've been to and perhaps which factories they've visited. But of course that's private company information and nobody is just going to tell them that without raising red flags. So the hacker needs to trick the information from them. It's not hard to imagine the process.

> Hacker: Hi, I'm Dr. Jones, and I'm calling from the school about your daughter Nancy.

> Target: Oh really? What has she done now?

Hacker: Well, she's got a persistent nosebleed we can't get to stop. I'd like to ask you about any chemicals she's been exposed to, manufacturing chemicals and such. These symptoms are rare except in people exposed to these chemicals. Can you tell me anything?

Target: (spills their guts)

This is not really illegal in most places but it causes unneeded stress. Not to mention it's just mean to make a parent worry like that.

Hacking to Take Over Your World

Hacking isn't just about interactions. You know that. Some people say politics is about interactions. Maybe. But you probably thought hacking is about breaking security. Sometimes it is. What it's really about is taking control of something or changing it as well. Understanding interactions and what they mean in the real world, using the basic terms we've discussed, is useful when you're trying to infiltrate, discover, or even invent. Why would you do this? To have the freedom to make something you own do what you want. And to keep others from changing something you own in the name of what some people might call security (but we're not those people).

Sometimes you buy something and the company you bought it from will attempt to forcefully or sneakily make sure you can't customize it or change it beyond their rules. And you can agree to that, as long as you accept the fact that if you break it then you can't expect them to fix it or replace it. So hacking something you own does more than make it yours, it makes it irrevocably and undeniably yours. As scary as that may sound to some, it certainly has its advantages. Especially if you want to keep others out of your stuff.

For many, many people (we could put many more "manys" here to get the point across that we really mean "way way too many"), security is about putting a product in place, whether that's a lock or an alarm or a firewall or anything that theoretically keeps them secure. But sometimes those products don't work as well they should, or come with their own problems that just increase your **Attack Surface**, when a security product should be shrinking it. (The Attack Surface is all the ways, all the interactions, that allow for something or someone to be attacked.) And good luck getting that product improved in a mass-marketing, pay-as-you-go, crowd-sourcing, "you bought it as-is and that's what you have to live with" kind of world. That's why you hack your security. You need to analyze the product and figure out where it fails and how to change it so it works better. Then you might have to hack it some more to keep that company you bought it from, from changing it back to the default!

So when you think of hacking in terms of breaking security, remember that's just one area that hacking is useful for, because without being able to do that, you may have to give up some freedom or some privacy that you don't want to give up. (And yes we get it that you may not care right now about certain things you do or say or post, but the Internet has a long memory and it's getting better and better at helping others recall those memories of you. What goes on the net stays on the net. So consider this for the future you even if the you of today doesn't care.)

Now that you get the idea about interactions, let's get into them into more detail. You know the basic interactions as Access and Trust but have you heard of **Visibility**? That's the third type of interaction. It's just as powerful as the other two. In police language, it's simplified as *opportunity* but in hacking it's more about knowing if there is something to interact with or not. This interaction brings along a whole lot of new security techniques like deception, illusion, and camouflage, as well as all-new hacking techniques for avoiding and getting around security measures like deception, illusion, and camouflage!

When famous bank robber Jesse James was asked why he robbed banks, he said it's because that's where the money is. What he meant is that through Visibility he knew that the banks had money where other things he could rob might not. Banks have Visibility: people know what assets they hold. But not everything has Visibility. As a matter of fact Privacy is the opposite of Visibility and it's a powerful way to avoid being a target. Whether on dangerous streets, in the jungle, or on the Internet, keeping a low **Exposure** and avoiding Visibility is a way to keep from getting attacked in the first place.

Exercises

The Internet is so popular for creating myths and perpetuating false stories that it's hard to know what's real information and what is just a hoax. So if you want to learn to be a good hacker, get in the habit of checking your facts and learning the truth about things. That's why you're going to search and find out if Jesse James really did say that. And don't go easy on the answer by just going to the first web page you find, dig for it!

Now that you're getting used to looking things up, find the truth about these common things:

1.5   In the Inuit language where the word igloo comes from, but what does it really mean? What did you have to search for to find the answer?

1.6   Many parents are quick to point out that sugar makes little kids hyper-active but does it really? What interactions are really occurring in their little bellies when children eat a lot of candy or sugary foods that make them act silly and hyper?

1.7   You might have heard that sugar causes cavities (caries) in your teeth but what is the real interaction that takes place – what really causes it? Is it sugar or not? Bonus points if you can say what brushing is as an interaction to fight the real cause and find the name of at least one of the chemicals that addresses the root of the problem (*hint: fluoride is wrong*).

 Game On: A Hacker's First Toy

It was a cool afternoon at Jace's grandparents' apartment. Rain slammed down onto the outside world but didn't bother anyone in the building. The ten-year-old always enjoyed spending time with her grandfather because he enjoyed spending time with her. Her mother had woven her fine dark hair into a singe ponytail with a pink bow at the end. Three hours into playing and the pink bow was sideways and barely holding on to a few strands of hair. Jace was busy finding things to play with around the small home when she came across one of her favorite toys.

This particular toy was a small handmade box slimmer than a shoe box made of painted wood. There was a crank handle on one end. On the top of the box there was a small wooden wall with a tiny hole, a sleeping cat and a sleeping wooden old lady sitting in a chair. When Jace turned the box handle a mouse appeared from a hole in the wall and moved towards the sleeping cat. Once the mouse arrived at the cat, the cat leaped into the air and landed on top the sleeping ladies head. The surprised wooden lady would open her eyes and kick out her legs as the mouse watched in amusement.

Jace would wind the handle backwards to reset the automata machine and as soon as the mouse was hidden back in the wall, turn the handle forward to create the whole comical scene again. The ten-year-old would usually do this a few times before getting bored and turn her attention to something else. However, this time Grandpa was watching Jace and paying close attention to her expression. Jace didn't seem satisfied with just watching the mouse spook the cat and watching the cat land on the little woman's head. *She wonders how it works,* he thought, and decided to give her a surprise.

Crouching next to Jace in his gray work pants, he pushed his glasses back. He said, "I see you like the mouse causing all the trouble here. It is because the mouse is the smallest of the creatures in the cast or because the mouse is sneaky enough to surprise the cat and the woman in the chair?"

Jace didn't look behind her because she knew the smell of her grandfather and he always asked questions like this. His closeness to her made her feel comfortable but she didn't know the answer to his question. She had her own question but didn't know what that question was or how to ask it. She continued to turn the handle in both directions to see how each piece was moving. She answered into the air, "I don't understand how all the parts move. I like this but I wish I could see what's happening inside, what makes everything work."

Grandpa clapped his hands in delight. This was the moment he had been waiting years for, the moment Jace pushed her curiosity into his realm. Without getting up, Grandpa pivoted around on the orange carpet to sit next to the child. He gently pulled the toy away from her small hands and asked, "What if you can't open the box to look inside? What will you do?"

Jace studied the wooded container and simply said, "I'll break it open, then."

Grandpa's eyebrows knitted and he stared at Jace, who went wide-eyed. "This toy doesn't belong to you. You can play with it but you can't just go around breaking things that don't belong to you. If you want to see how it works, you need to find another way to do it. Criminals break things on purpose. You, my dear, are not a criminal. You are curious about things so I'm going to show you how to be a hacker."

Jace knew what a criminal was but had never heard of a hacker before. She squared her shoulders and sat up straight since this was turning into one of Grandpa's teaching talks. These were always fun. She asked her grandfather, "What's a hacker?"

"A hacker is someone who wants to learn how machines work. They read about them, build them, play with them. Hacking … at least when I was growing up, hacking didn't mean anything illegal. There are people who call themselves hackers but they're really criminals because they steal from other people, destroy things that don't belong to them and hurt other people. Real hackers don't."

Child eyes looking into Grandpa's, Jace said, "Like when I said I would break the box open, that's something a bad person would do." She nodded: no remorse for her previous statement, just taking in the difference between one type of action versus another. The gray haired gentleman moved the box in his hands until he felt a spot on the bottom of the toy. Using his thumbnail, he carefully slide the side panel upwards to reveal in the inside of the box. Turning the box over, he did the same thing to open the other side panel.

The ten-year-old stared into the inner workings of this machine. Grandpa smiled, he watching her tilting the box and looking in from every angle. Inside were wooden gears, cams, a worm drive and small fishing rod weights: no longer a toy but a spectacular invention of moving parts. It reminded Jace of Grandpa's old pocket watch, with all the delicate gears and springs you could see in the back.

Grandpa said, "Go on, touch it. Move the pieces to see what happens. Watch how each piece makes other parts move. Check out the cat and mouse. What makes them move?"

Jace was baffled by the puzzle of motion in her hands. She reached into the exposed box and touched the pin wheel. A pin fell off the wheel and landed somewhere inside the box. When Jace tried to turn the crank, the mouse moved but the cat didn't. She looked up at Grandpa, stricken: the toy was broken!

Grandpa looked at Jace and softly said, "No, no, no. It isn't broken. We just have to put the pin back on the wheel. Well, we first have to find the pin. Shake the box until you hear something loose rattle around."

The child gently jiggled the box, then titled it up and down until the pin fell on to the carpet in front of her. Grandpa continued, "See, if we do accidentally break something it is our duty as hackers to fix it. If we come across something that's already broken, we either let the owner know it's broken or we fix it and tell the owner how we fixed it. We have to be responsible citizens, as hackers and as good people."

Jace handed the pin to her grandfather who handed the pin right back to Jace. He said, "You broke it, you fix it. I'll show you how."

He picked up the machine and took it over to the kitchen table where the light was better. Jace followed him and pulled up a chair alongside her mentor. Grandpa pulled a pencil out of his breast pocket and laid the box on its side so they could see the insides.

"See the crank handle on the outside of the box," he began. "When you turn that handle in one direction the mouse comes out of the wall and moves towards the cat. The mouse is moved because below the box surface, the mouse sits on a hidden track that is kind of like a corkscrew. The handle you turn causes the corkscrew track, what is called a worm drive, to rotate the mouse forward and also turn a pin wheel at the end of the track. The pin wheel has four pins on it."

Grandpa pointed his pencil at the pinwheel that was missing one pin. Jace opened up her small hand to reveal the lone pin. He continued, "You turn the crank four times and each time the mouse moves forward and the pin wheel makes one turn of a pin. Once the pinwheel moves four rotations, there is a cam connected to the fourth pin. It's called a drop cam even though it's shaped like an egg or a pear. The fourth rotation causes the drop cam to move to its highest point, which is connected to the cat."

Jace was looking at each mechanism but wasn't sure she understood how they worked together. Her grandfather moved his pencil to the cat, which rested on a wire hook. "See, when the drop cam hits its highest point on the fourth rotation, the wire is released and the cat jumps into the air on a curved path. The cat lands on the little woman's head. Now, if you look closely, you'll see the sitting lady has two buttons on top of her head. When the cat lands on her head, the cat pushed down on the two buttons in her hair. One button cause the woman's eyes to open and the other button causes her legs to pop forward in surprise."

Grandpa started the box at the first stage to show how a single turn on the crank made the worm drive push the mouse towards the cat and also move the pin wheel one rotation. This one rotation caused the drop cam to turn a quarter of a rotation. A second turn of the crank caused the mouse to move closer to the cat and the pin wheel rotated one more time, which made the drop cam complete a half rotation. The third crank turn did the same thing as the previous two turns. It wasn't until the forth crank turn that the mouse reached the cat, which turned the pin wheel to the fourth position. This also cause the drop cam to move to its highest point and released the cat. The cat flew on the wire and landed on the little woman's head as she sat sleeping in her chair.

The cat landed on the woman's head, the buttons pushed, that opened her eyes and made her legs swing out in surprise. Turning the crank in the opposite direction reset all the movements. Jace watched intently as she turned the handle slowly in one direction and then the other direction. Grandpa rested back in his kitchen chair and watched as Jace's mind absorbed all this mechanical movement information.

With her teacher looking on, Jace removed a pin or a part to see how that changed the toy's mechanics. Each change either had disastrous results or no effect at all. Several hours into the toy tinkering Jace began to ask a series of questions.

"Why not use a magnet instead?"

"How come the cat hangs on a wire when a spring would work better?"

"What happens if I turn the crank five or six times?"

"Why is a worm drive thing here, when you could use a curved track instead?"

"Does this work upside down?"

Grandpa interrupted Jace by raising his index finger to his lips. He looked with wonder in his eyes and repeated, "Why is a worm drive used when a curved track could be used instead? Is that what you just said?"

Jace nodded as she explored the pinwheel closer. Grandpa grabbed a piece of paper and started to draw on it. When he was done drawing a few drafts he slid the paper over to his granddaughter and asked, "Is that what you mean by a curved track?"

Jace took a quick look and said, "Yeah but you need to add a small piece to the mouse to keep it on the track. It would be smoother that way and easier to build."

Grandpa's mouth worked but he said nothing.

Jace added, "Plus you can get rid of the pin wheel by cutting a slot at the end of the track. One less thing to go wrong. You won't need to turn the crank four times, either. When the mouse gets to the end of the track, the slot will trigger the wire to release. You can get rid of the drop cam too. Less parts to build. And why have two buttons on the top of the woman's head. Ya only need one to open her eyes and make her legs pop out."

Grandpa's pencil hit paper and scribbled fast as he thought, *I just got schooled.*

Game Over

The Four Point Process

When you take the three types of interactions together, you have **Porosity**, the basis of an Attack Surface. And like the word implies, it's the pores or "holes" in any defenses you have to have in order for any necessary interactions to take place (as well as any unknown or unnecessary interactions taking place). For instance, a store still needs to put products on the shelves so people can touch them, put them in a cart and buy them. These are the interactions they need to sell things. But they might not be aware of the employees who are sneaking stuff out of the loading dock, which is an interaction that they don't want.

Porosity is something you need to know about to protect yourself or attack some target. But it's not enough to analyze something to hack it. To do that you need to know something deeper about the three types of interactions you just learned. This is another little secret from the OSSTMM and it's called the **Four Point Process (FPP)**. It outlines four ways these interactions are used to analyze something as deeply as possible, and by analyze we mean to mess with it so we can watch it and see what happens.

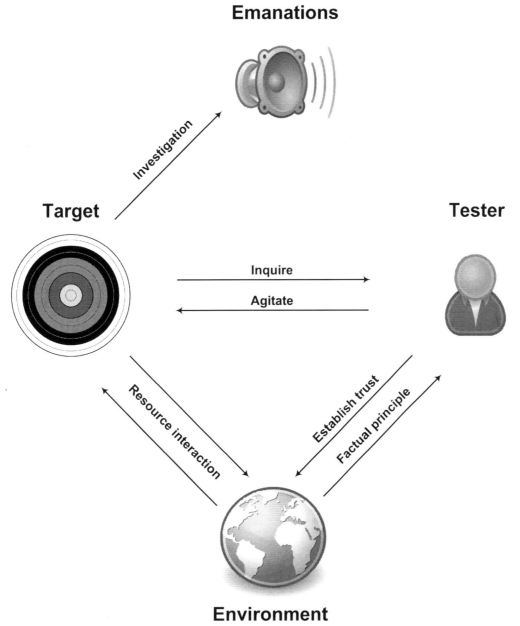

Figure 1.1: The Four Point Process

The Echo Process

We grow up discovering things and learning things by interacting with them directly. Little kids poke the dried-up squirrel with a stick to see if it's dead. This is called the **echo process**. It's the most basic and immature form of analysis. It's like yelling into a cave and listening for the response. The echo process requires throwing different types of Access interactions at a target and then monitoring its reactions to figure out what ways you can interact with it. The echo process is a cause-and-effect type of verification.

This is an odd way to test something, because although it makes for a very fast test, it also isn't very accurate. For instance, when using the echo process in testing security, a target that does not respond is considered secure. That's the same as not having Visibility. But we also know that just because something is non-responsive to a particular type of interaction that doesn't mean it's "secure." If this were true then opossums would never get killed by other animals when they played dead and everyone would be safe from bear attacks just by passing out in fear. But it's just not true. Avoiding Visibility might help you survive some types of interactions but certainly not all.

Unfortunately, the majority of ways people investigate things in their everyday life is through the echo process alone. There is so much information lost in this kind of one-dimensional analysis that we should be thankful the health care industry has evolved past the "Does it hurt if I do this?" method of diagnosis. If hospitals only used the echo process to determine the health of a person they would rarely truly help people. On the bright side the waiting room times would be very short. That's why some doctors, most scientists, and especially hackers use the Four Point Process to make sure they don't miss anything.

The Four Point Process has you look at interactions in the following ways:

1. **Induction**: What can we tell about the target from its environment? How does it behave in that environment? If the target is not influenced by its environment, that's interesting too.

2. **Inquest**: What signals (emanations) does the target give off? Investigate any tracks or indicators of those emanations. A system or process generally leaves a signature of interactions with its environment.

3. **Interaction**: What happens when you poke it? This point calls for echo tests, including expected and unexpected interactions with the target, to trigger responses.

4. **Intervention**: How far will it bend before it breaks? Intervene with the resources the target needs, like electricity, or meddle with its interactions with other systems to understand the extremes under which it can continue operating.

Back to our hospital example...the four stages of the FPP would look like this:

1. The **interaction** function is the echo process where the doctors poke the patients, talk to them, and test their reflexes on the elbows and knees and use other tools of the "Does it hurt if I do this?" method.

2. The **inquest** is reading **emanations** from the patient like pulse, blood pressure, and brain waves.

3. The **intervention** is changing or stressing the patient's homeostasis, behavior, routine, or comfort level to see what happens.

4. And finally **induction**, which is examining the environment, the places where the person visited before they got ill and how they may have affected the patient, such as what they may have touched, ingested, or breathed.

Exercise

1.8 As you can see, the Four Point Process lets you more deeply investigate interactions. Now you can try it. Explain how you would use the Four Point Process to know if a clock is working – and then if it's working correctly by keeping the right time.

What to Hack

When you're hacking anything you need to set up some ground rules. You need the language and the concepts to know what you're actually hacking. The **Scope** is a word we use to describe the total possible operating environment, which is every interaction that the thing you want to hack has.

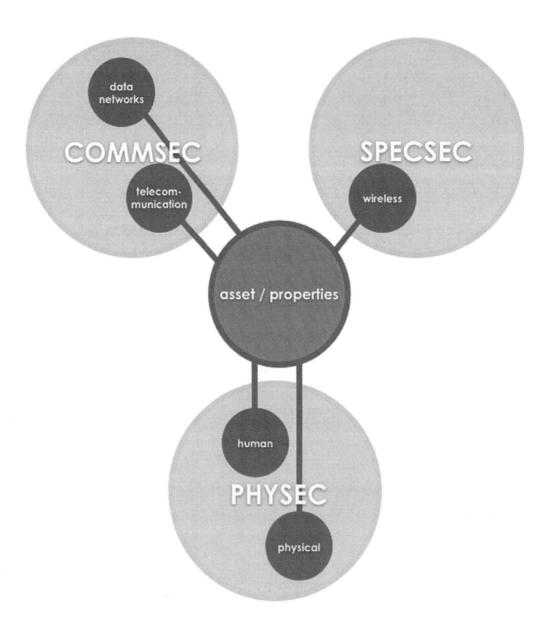

Figure 1.2: Scope

Feed Your Head: Classes and Channels

In professional terminology (also useful to hackers), the Scope is made up of three **Classes** that subdivide to five **Channels**:

Class	Channel
Physical Security (PHYSSEC)	Human
	Physical
Spectrum Security (SPECSEC)	Wireless
Communications Security (COMSEC)	Telecommunications
	Data Networks

Classes are not something you have to be too worried about but they are the official labels used currently in the security industry, government, and the military. Classes define an area of study, investigation, or operation. So if you're looking up more information on any topic, it's really good to know what the pros call it.

Channels are the common terms for the ways you interact with assets. It's not uncommon to hack a gadget by using the Four Point Process over each Channel. Yes it seems like a lot of work, but think of how thrilling it is when you discover a way to make it work that's not listed in any manual, or better yet not even known to the manufacturer!

An **Asset** can be anything that has value to the owner. It can be physical property like gold, people, blueprints, laptops, the typical 900 MHz frequency phone signal, and money; or intellectual property such as personnel data, a relationship, a brand, business processes, passwords, and something said over the 900 MHz phone signal.

Dependencies are the things beyond the asset owner's ability to provide independently. Not many computer owners generate their own electricity, for instance. Even if it's not likely someone will cut off your electricity, it is still within your scope.

The goal of security is **Separation** between an asset as well as its dependencies, and any threat to them.

We say **security is a function of separation**. There are four ways we can create this separation:
- Move the asset to create a barrier between it and the threats.
- Change the threat to a harmless state.
- Destroy the threat.
- Destroy the asset. (Not recommended!)

When we're hacking we look for places where interactions with the target are possible, and where they are not. Think of doors into a building. Some are necessary for workers; others are necessary for customers. Some may be needed to escape fire. And some may not be necessary at all.

Every door, though, is a point of interaction, one that aids both necessary operations and unwanted ones like theft. When we come on the scene as hackers, we don't start out knowing the reasons for all these interactive points, so we analyze them with the Four Point Process.

Consider the example of a guy who wants to be totally safe from lightning. The only way to do this (while still on Earth) is to get into a mountain where it is completely impossible for lightning to get inside through all that dirt and rock. Assuming he never needs to go out again we can say his security is absolutely 100%. But if we start drilling holes in the mountain the lightning has one more point of access with every hole, and the porosity increases. The OSSTMM differentiates between being **Safe** from lightning and being **Secure** from it. The simple fact is that the more porosity there is, the more likely a hacker can make changes and control what they want.

Visibility

Access

Trust

**No Porosity
(100% security)**

Figure 1.3: Porosity

Feed Your Head: Porosity	
Here are some examples that describe how pores can be located, classified, and determined in the hacking process.	
Term	**Definition**
Visibility	When police investigate a crime, they look for *means, motive* and *opportunity*. If an asset is visible, it can be attacked, but if it's not visible, it can't be targeted – though it could be discovered. Some security professionals like to say that **obfuscation** is poor security because it doesn't protect anything, it only hides it. But that's not a bad thing especially since you don't always need a permanent security answer. To that effect the **OSSTMM** offers this little gem: *"Security doesn't have to last forever, just longer than anything else that might notice it's gone."*
Access	Access is the number of different places where interactions can occur to the outside of the scope. For a building this could be doors to the street or windows and for a server on the Internet it could be the number of open network ports or services available on that computer.

Trust	Trust is when one entity accepts free interaction with another entity within the scope. It's why you don't ask your mother for ID when she comes to hug you. It's also why you don't suspect she's poisoned your food. You learn to trust the things inside your scope. Then one day if she gets taken over by an alien race and replaced (a lá **Invasion of the Body Snatchers**) and does poison your food you'll eat it unsuspectingly. Thus trust is both a security hole and a common replacement for authentication, the way we can validate if someone is who we think they are. Trust is a strange topic because it's such a human thing to do and pretty valuable in society. Without trust, we'd never be able to interact freely. But because of trust, we are easily tricked, fooled, robbed, and lied to. OSSTMM research on trust shows that there are 10 reasons to trust someone called **Trust Properties** and if all ten reasons are satisfied then we can trust safely without any worry. But that same research shows that most people need only one trust reason to be satisfied and the really paranoid or cynical are okay with just three reasons to trust.

Resources

Effective research, learning and critical thinking are key skills for a hacker. Hacking, in reality, is a creative process that is based more on lifestyle than lesson. We can't teach you everything that you need to know, but we can help you recognize what you need to learn. Because science advances so quickly, what we teach today may not be relevant tomorrow. It is much better for you to embrace hacker learning habits, which are probably the most vital part of hacking, and which will separate you from the **script kiddie** (a hacker word that means a person who uses tools without really knowing how or why they work).

If you run into a word or concept you don't understand in this lesson, it's essential you look it up. Ignoring new words will only make it difficult for you to understand concepts in the coming lessons. You'll be asked to investigate a topic and then expected to use the information that you find to complete the exercises in that lesson – but those lessons won't explain to you how to do this research. So be sure to spend as much time as you need learning to use the various resources available to you.

Books

You might be surprised that we don't point you straight at the Internet, but books are a great way to learn the foundation and factual science of everything you want to explore. Want to know something about computer science, like the hardware details of your PC? Nothing will help you more than reading a current book on the subject. The main problem with books for computers is that they become out-of-date very quickly. The secret is to learn to see the fundamental structure underneath the thin skin of details. MS-DOS and Windows are clearly different, but both are based on principles of Boolean logic that have driven computers since Ada, Countess of Lovelace, wrote the first computer programs in the nineteenth century. Security and privacy concerns may have changed in the last 2,500 years, but **The Art of War** by Sun Tzu covers fundamental principles that still apply today. (By the way, there is no faster way to look like a **n00b** than by quoting Sun Tzu. Some things you should know how to apply but not say. And quoting The Art of War proves that you didn't really read The Art of War because Sun Tzu even says to keep your real knowledge a secret.)

Even though information found in books may not be as up to date as information that comes from other sources, the information you find in books is more likely to be better written than most other sources. Sometimes they are more accurate too. A writer who spends a year writing a book is more likely to check facts than someone who is updating a blog six times a day. (See the Sections on Zines and Blogs for more information.)

But remember – accurate does not mean unbiased. The sources of the author's information themselves might be biased. "History books are written by the winners" (look up that quote), and the same holds true when the politics and social norms of the time may prevent certain information from being published. This commonly happens with school textbooks that are chosen through a political process and contain only the information considered socially acceptable to know. Don't think you've found a golden truth just because you read it in a book. The truth is that anyone can write a book and any book can contain anyone's version of the truth.

Don't look at a book and give up before you even start just because it's so big. Nobody reads most of these massive books that you see sitting around from cover to cover. **Think of them as prehistoric web pages.** Open one up to a random page and begin to read. If you don't understand something, go backward and look for the explanation (or skip forward to something that does make sense). Jump through the book, backwards and forwards, just as you would bounce from link to link in a web page. This type of non-linear research is often much more interesting and satisfying for hackers, since it's about satisfying your curiosity more than it is about reading.

Finally, one thing that book readers gain as a valuable skill is the ability to write well. This is a huge advantage whenever you are trying to understand and participate in a new field. It also makes what you have to say more credible to other readers, especially those who are in positions of authority.

Magazines and Newspapers

Magazines and newspapers are highly useful for providing concise, timely information. Both types of publications can be very short on details, though. Also be aware that every newspaper or magazine has its own audience and its own agenda or theme, regardless of any claims of being "fair and unbiased." Know the theme of the publication: a Linux magazine isn't necessarily a good source of information about Microsoft Windows, because Windows is a conflicting theme (a competing operating system), and frankly a Linux magazine's readers want to read about the superiority of Linux. Many of the specialty magazines employ **cherry picking,** the technique of highlighting only the positive aspects of something fitting the magazine's theme or highlighting only the negative aspects of the things that don't.

Be aware of a publication's possible biases. That's where they give you opinions instead of facts or leave out facts from a story to fit their own opinions or so you can't form your own opinion. Consider the source! Even "neutral" appearing periodicals can be full of biases and speculation, a nice way of saying "educated guesses" but is more often just "guesses" on the part of the journalist.

There's is a huge movement in the medical field to have all medical and pharmaceutical trials published (or at least all publicly-funded trials) even if they failed so that doctors can make even more informed choices about what medicine and procedures to apply. While current medical journals may be publishing "facts" from research trials, the details and circumstances behind those facts are still cloudy. That's really important when you deal with subjects that rely on having root causes. Causation requires that the cause precedes and is the reason for the effect.

Other tricks used by periodicals (both inadvertently and purposely) are **anecdotal evidence**, which is opinions from people published as evidence regardless of whether they are experts or not; **authoritative evidence**, in which industry employees represented as experts give their opinions, or people who are authorities in one area offer their opinion in another area in which they have no expertise; and finally, **speculation**, dressing up something as true because "everyone" believes it is true, though there's no actual attribution to anyone specific.

The best way to deal with the issues of accuracy and agenda is to be well and widely read. If you read about an interesting issue in a magazine, look into it further. Take one side of the issue, and look for confirmations; then take the other side, and look for rebuttals. Some cultures do this by default. It's part of their social habits to seek other sides to the story. That's a really powerful cultural trait, especially if you're trying to assure a successful democracy.

Exercises

1.9   Search the Internet for three online magazines on the subject of hacking. How did you find these magazines? How do you know they are telling facts?

1.10 Are all three magazines specifically about computer hacking? What else do they offer that might be helpful in other fields or other businesses?

Feed Your Head: Speculation

The following paragraph is from a newspaper article about a robbery. Can you find the *speculation*? Mark the areas that you suspect:

The Lake Meadow Bank and Mortgage Lender was robbed Tuesday afternoon when masked gunmen walked in just moments before closing and held the employees hostage for an hour before what appears to be making their getaway in a late model SUV. None of the hostages were reportedly injured.

No one could identify the gunmen which leads the police to believe that this may have been a professional job as moments after the robbery, the car was spotted behind the bank and heading south towards the dense woods of the Bluegreen Mountains. The police are now likely to be looking for experienced robbers who may have prison records and who also have relationships to people living in that area.

With an average of 57 thefts at banks being reported every day within this country and the Bluegreen county population reportedly to reach a population of over 50,000 by next year, this could be the start of a rash of bank robberies from that region. "This looks like the start of a trend." said the police commissioner, Smith.

Did you find any *speculation*? You should have! But it's okay if you didn't. We are becoming more desensitized to speculation because there's so much of it so it's hard for us to recognize it. If this trend continues maybe in the future all our news might just come from a single journalist *speculating* on news stories as they happen. In the short example above, there is actually only one real fact written in that whole story. The only fact is that a bank had been robbed on Tuesday afternoon.

Now for the sake of obviousness, this is what it would look like if we changed all the speculation to make it more ridiculously obvious:

The Righteous Bank and Mortgage Lender was robbed Tuesday afternoon when what appears to be masked chickens walked in just days before closing which means they could have held the employees buck naked for as long as a second before what appears to be making their get-away in a hot air balloon shaped like a giant cow. None of the hostages were reportedly covered in feathers.

No one could identify the chickens which leads the police to believe that they may have had a professional disguise artist among them in addition to an accomplished balloon animal maker as moments after the robbery, a hot air balloon was spotted above the bank and flying south towards Antarctica. The police are now likely to be looking for accomplished make-up artists who also have ties to balloon animal hobbyists.

With an average of 57 thefts at banks being reported every day within this country and the ballooning industry reporting sales to reach $47 gazillion by some future date, this could be the start of a rash of bank robberies using farm-animal-shaped balloons. "This looks like the start of a trend." said the police commissioner, Gordon.

With the overwhelming use of speculation and statistics across all industries it is no wonder that it has entered the security industry with such force. The commonly used term in this industry is **FUD** which is an acronym for **Fear, Uncertainty, and Doubt**. It is how speculation is used in security to gain attention for one's interests and sell security solutions. Unfortunately it plays very well with the primitive paranoia in the human psyche and a growing numbness to speculation. This has led to some really bad security products and bad security analysis in the security industry.

Search Engines

Google is a well known search engine but it's not the only search engine. Bing is very good with searches in the form of simple questions and Yahoo is good for doing thorough research. Be very aware that all these web services want to know everything they can about you, and probably know more than they should. They will record your searches and which websites you visit after you search.

There are engines like DuckDuckGo.com that may give you some – or a lot – of anonymity, which might be a good thing when you are looking into dark corners.

Websites are searchable while they're online and usually long after that. Typically they're preserved in the form of **cached pages**. An Internet cache is an online record of past versions of websites, or even of websites that have gone dark. Search engines and archive sites keep this information indefinitely, which in Internet terms is "forever." That's a valuable thing to remember before you ever put anything on the Internet: it isn't going away. Ever. You may have to look for a link to the cached copy of a page. Google, for instance, used to put a simple link labeled "Cache" alongside the regular link to a result. That has changed to a fly-out menu on the right, and may have changed again by the time you read this.

Besides the search engines, there are also useful public caches at places like the **Internet Archive at http://www.archive.org**. You can find cached versions of whole websites from over the years, which can be very useful for finding information that has "disappeared."

One final note on websites: don't assume you can trust a website just because it shows up in a search engine. Many hacker attacks and viruses are spread just by visiting a website or downloading innocent-looking programs, screen savers or any shared files. You can safeguard yourself by not downloading programs from untrusted websites, and by making sure your browser runs in a **sandbox**. But this may not be enough. A browser is a window to the Internet and like any window, bad stuff can float in just because it's open. Sometimes you won't even know until it's too late.

Exercises

1.11 There are many search engines out there. Some are good for getting to the **Invisible Web**, areas of the Internet that are hard for most search engines to dig through, like certain private databases. A good researcher knows how to use them all. Some websites specialize in tracking search engines. So find five search engines you haven't used or maybe even heard of before.

1.12 There are also search engines that search other search engines. These are called **meta search engines**. Find one of these meta search engines.

1.13 Search for "security and hacking" (including the quotation marks) and note the top three answers. How do the results differ when you DON'T use quotes?

1.14 It is very different to search for a topic than it is to search for a word or phrase. In the previous exercise, you searched for a phrase. Now you will search for an idea.

To do this, **think of phrases that might be on the page you're looking for**. If you want the search engine to give you a list of online magazines about hacking, you won't get far by searching for "a list of online magazines about hacking." Not many web pages will contain that phrase! You'll get some hits but not many.

Instead, you need to think, "If I was setting up a hacking magazine, what would a typical sentence in that magazine look like?" Put the following words and phrases into a search engine and find out which provides the best results for your search:

1. my list of favorite magazines on hacking

2. list of professional hacking magazines

3. resources for hackers

4. hacking magazine

5. magazines hacking security list resources

1.15 Find the oldest website from Mozilla in the Internet Archive. To do this you need to search on "www.mozilla.org" at the http://www.archive.org website.

1.16 Now to put it all together, let's say you want to download version 1 of the Netscape web browser. Using search engines and the Internet Archives, see if you can locate and download version 1.

Websites and Web Applications

The *de facto* standard for sharing information is currently through a web browser. While we classify everything we see as "the web," more and more what we really use are "web applications," since not everything on the web is a website. If you check email using a web browser, or get music through a web-connected service, you are using a web application.

Sometimes web applications require privileges. This means you need a login name and password to get access. Having access when you have a legal right to access is called having **privileges**. Hacking into a website to change a page may mean you have access, but since you have no legal right to be there, you don't have privileged access. As you continue to use the web, you'll find that many places give access to privileged areas by accident.

When you find something like this, it's a good habit to report it to the website administrator. However, beware of potential legal repercussions. Unfortunately, many administrators frown upon unsolicited vulnerability reports.

To contribute to making the Internet a safer place while also protecting yourself, you should consider using an **anonymizer** service (e.g., TOR or anonymous remailers, etc.) for sending out vulnerability reports to these administrators. But be aware: all of these anonymous technologies have their weak points and you may not be as anonymous as you think you are! (More than one hacker has learned this the hard way.)

Exercises

1.17 Use a search engine to find sites that have made the mistake of giving privileged access to everyone. To do this, we'll look for folders that let us list the contents (a "directory listing"), something that usually shouldn't be allowed. For this we will use some Google command tricks at http://www.google.com. Enter this into the search box:

```
allintitle:"index of" .js
```

Scan the results and you may find one that looks like a directory listing. This type of searching is known as Google Hacking.

1.18 Can you find other types of documents in this way? Find three more directory listings that contain .xls files, .doc files, and .avi files.

1.19 Are there other search options like "allintitle:"? How can you find them?

Zines

Zines, also known as **e-zines**, are the descendants of **fanzines**: small, usually free magazines with a very small distribution (less than 10,000 readers) and often produced by hobbyists and amateur journalists. Fanzines were printed on paper. Zines on the Internet, like the famous **2600** or the **Phrack** web zine, are written by volunteers; often that means the producers don't edit content for non-technical errors. Sometimes strong language can be surprising for those who aren't familiar with this genre.

> Zines have very strong themes or agendas, and tend to be very opinionated. However, they are also more likely to show and argue both sides of issues, since they usually don't care about or have to please advertisers and subscribers.

Exercises

1.20 Search the Internet for three zines on the subject of hacking. How did you find these zines?

1.21 Why do you classify these as zines? Remember, just because they market it as a zine or put "zine" in the title doesn't mean it is one.

Blogs

A **blog** can be considered an evolution of the zine, usually with a writing staff of one. Blogs are updated more often than most print publications or zines, and create communities tied to very strong themes. It's as important to read the commentary as the postings. Even more so than zines, on blogs the response is often immediate and opinionated, with comments from every side. This is one of their special values.

> There are millions of blogs on the Internet, but only a small percentage of them are active. The information on almost all, however, is still available.

Exercises

1.22 Search the Internet for three blogs on the subject of hacking.

1.23 What groups or communities are these associated with?

1.24 Is there a security, law enforcement or academic theme to the blog?

Forums and Mailing Lists

Forums and **mailing lists** are communally developed media, a lot like a recording of conversations at a party. Be a little skeptical about everything you read there. The conversations shift focus often, a lot of what is said is rumor, some people are **trolling**, a **flame war** might erupt, and, when the party is over, no one is certain who said what. Forums and mailing lists are similar, because there are many ways for people to contribute inaccurate information – sometimes intentionally – and there are ways for people to contribute anonymously or as someone else. Since topics and themes change quickly, to get all the information it's important to read the whole thread of comments and not just the first few.

You can find forums on almost any topic, and many online magazines and newspapers offer forums for readers to write responses to the articles they publish. Because of this, forums are invaluable for getting more than one opinion on an article; no matter how much one person liked it, there is certain to be someone who didn't.

> There are many mailing lists on special topics, but they can be hard to find. Sometimes the best technique is to search for information on a particular subject to find a mailing list community that deals with it.

As a hacker, what is most important for you to know is that many forums and mailing lists are not searchable through major search engines. While you might find a forum or list through a search engine, you may not find information on individual posts. This information is part of the invisible web because it contains data that is only searchable directly on the website or forum.

Exercises

1.25 Find two hacker forums. How did you find these forums?

a. Can you determine the themes or topics of specialty of these websites?

b. Do the topics in the forums reflect the theme of the website hosting them?

1.26 Find two hacking or security mailing lists.

a. Who is the "owner" of these lists? Can you see the member list? (You might need to figure out the application the list has been developed on and then search the web for the hidden commands to see the list of members on that kind of mailing list.)

b. On which lists would you expect the information to be more factual and less opinionated? Why?

Newsgroups

Newsgroups have been around a long time. There were newsgroups long before the World Wide Web existed. Google purchased the entire archive of newsgroups and put them online at http://groups.google.com. Newsgroups are like mailing list archives but without the mail. People posted there directly like they do when commenting to a website. You will find posts in there from the early 1990s onward.

Like the web archives, the group archives can be important for finding who really originated an idea or created a product. They're also useful for finding obscure information that never may have made it to a web page.

Newsgroups aren't used any less today than they were years ago, before the web became the mainstream for sharing information. However, they also haven't grown as their popularity is replaced by new web services like blogs and forums.

Exercises

1.27 Using Google's groups, find the oldest newsgroup posting you can on the subject of hacking.

1.28 Find other ways to use newsgroups. Are there applications you can use to read newsgroups?

1.29 How many newsgroups can you find that talk about hacking?

1.30 Can you find a current list of all the different newsgroups currently in existence?

Wikis

Wikis are a newer phenomenon on the Internet. Wikipedia (www.wikipedia.org) is probably the most famous one, but there are many others. Like many other sites wikis are put together by communities. Reports often claim that wikis are not accurate because they are contributed to by amateurs and fanatics. But that's true of books, mailing lists, magazines, and everything else too. What's important to know is that experts aren't the only source of great ideas or factual information. As the OSSTMM points out, facts come from the small steps of verifying ideas and not great leaps of discovery. That's why wikis are great sources of both professional and amateur ideas slowly and incrementally verifying each other.

Wikis will often discuss many sides of a topic and allow you to follow how information is argued, refuted, refined and changed through a list of edits. So they are great places to dig up information, but often you have to go to the wiki's website to do searches.

Exercises

1.31 Search for "Ada Lovelace." Do you see results from wikis?

1.32 Go to Wikipedia and repeat this search. Take a look at the article on her. Was it included in your search results?

1.33 Check out the edits of that Wikipedia page and look at the kinds of things that were corrected and changed. What kinds of things were changed? Was there anything changed and then changed back? Now pick a popular movie star or singer you like and go to that page in Wikipedia and check the edits. Do you notice a difference?

1.34 Find another wiki site and do the search again. Did any of the results show up in your original search engine search?

Social Media

Do you use a social media site? Or more than one? As a hacker you're well aware of the popular social media sites of the moment. How about the ones that aren't as hot as they used to be? They still exist, and all their data is still available, in most cases.

> This means there is a huge repository of information about us, most of which we have freely given away. And it's going to be there pretty much forever.

Social media sites often have sub-groups or communities of interest. Sites with a professional theme frequently have cybersecurity groups, and sites with an "underground" theme frequently have hacker groups. On the professional sites you are (and everyone else is) expected to use your real name. On the hacker sites, not so much.

Most important of all, do you use your real name on social media sites, or do you use a "handle?" Is there any way your handle could be traced to your real name? Most people don't realize it when they use handles, but it's not uncommon for them to accidentally or sometimes on purpose post their real names, address, city, school, jobs, and so on when using the handle. If another hacker DoXes your handle then they can usually pretty quickly figure out who you really are because of such small mistakes. If you use a handle to be anonymous to those who don't know you, then make sure you take measures to keep it that way. And NEVER confuse your handles if you have more than one.

Exercises

1.35 Search for yourself. Do you get any results (that are actually you)? Are any of them from social media sites?

1.36 Go to a social media site you use. Don't log in, but repeat the search as if you were an outsider. How much can you find out about yourself?

1.37 Go to a social media site a friend uses. Again, don't log in if you have an account. Search for your friend. How much can you find out about your friend?

Chat

Chat, which comes in the forms of **Internet Relay Chat (IRC)** and **Instant Messaging (IM)**, is a very popular way to communicate.

> As a research source, chat is extremely inconsistent because you're dealing with individuals in real time. Some will be friendly and some will be rude. Some will be harmless pranksters, but some will be malicious liars. Some will be intelligent and willing to share information, and some will be completely uninformed, but no less willing to share. It can be difficult to know which is which.

However, once you get comfortable with certain groups and channels, you may be accepted into the community. You will be allowed to ask more and more questions, and you will learn whom you can trust. Eventually you can get access to the very newest hacking exploits (also known as **zero day**, meaning it was just discovered right now) and advance your own knowledge.

Exercises

1.38 Find three instant messaging programs. What makes them different? Can they all be used to talk to each other?

1.39 Find out what IRC is and how you can connect to it. Can you discover what network holds ISECOM's channel? Once you join the network, how do you attach to the isecom-discuss channel?

1.40 How do you know what channels exist on an IRC network? Find three security channels and three hacker channels. Can you enter these channels? Are people talking or are they bots?

P2P

Peer to Peer, also known as **P2P**, is a network inside the Internet. Unlike the usual client/server network, where every computer communicates through a central server, the computers in a P2P network communicate directly with each other. Most people associate P2P with downloading MP3s and pirated movies on the infamous original Napster, but there are many other P2P networks – both for the purpose of exchanging information, and as a means of conducting research on distributed information sharing.

The problem with P2P networks is that, while you can find just about anything on them, some things are on the network illegally. And other things are there legally but the companies that created them still feel that they should not be there and are happy to demand money from the owner of any **Internet gateway** where it's downloaded.

At the moment there is not much agreement on whether the person whose Internet access was used to download content is responsible or if the police actually have to catch the person who did it. That's like saying that if your car is used to commit a crime the owner of the car, not the driver, goes to jail. Internet laws are currently not just and not fair so be extra careful!

Whether or not you are the kind of person who risks downloading intellectual property, there is no question that P2P networks can be a vital resource for finding information. Remember: there is nothing illegal about P2P networks – there are a lot of files that are available to be freely distributed under a wide variety of licenses – but there are also a lot of files on these networks that shouldn't be there. Don't be afraid to use P2P networks, but be aware of the dangers, and of what you are downloading.

Exercises

1.41 What are the three most popular and most used P2P networks? How does each one work? What program do you need to use it?

1.42 Research the protocol of one of those P2P networks. What does it do, and how does it make downloading faster?

1.43 Search for the words "download Linux." Can you download a distribution (or distro) of Linux using P2P?

Certifications

There are OSSTMM Security Tester and Security Analyst certifications, various colors of "hacker" certifications, certifications based on one version of "best practices" or another and certifications with all kinds of crazy initials or pieces of punctuation.

Why do you care about certifications? Because you can get some of them at any age, because you don't have to have a college degree to get them, and because they can put you in the position of the sought-after person, rather than the person asking for a gig.

The problem with best-practices based certifications is that best practices change often, because *best practices* is just another way of saying "what everyone else is doing right now."

Then there are research-based certifications, based on valid and repeatable research into human and system behavior. Needless to say our parent organization, ISECOM, falls squarely into the realm of research-based certification authorities. Whether from ISECOM or elsewhere, look for skills-based certifications and analysis-based or **applied knowledge** certifications that make you prove you can do what you say you've learned. That will be handy when you actually have to do it.

Seminars

Attending seminars is a great way to hear theory explained in detail and to watch skills in action. Even product-focused seminars are good to attend to see how a product is intended to be used, as long as you're aware that the event is a marketing pitch and their real job is to sell.

We would be remiss if we didn't mention that we can bring Hacker Highschool Seminars to many locations, and we can cover any of the available lessons. Seminars consist of professional hackers talking to students about hacking and being a hacker, both the bad and the good. These seminars take a sharp look at what real hackers are from research in the **Hacker Profiling Project**, a collaboration project with the United Nations to explore who hackers are and why they hack. Then you will go on to discover the bright side of hacking and how it's not always a dark thing.

One of the most powerful things we can help you find is the means to be as intellectually curious and resourceful as a hacker. Hackers succeed at what they do because they know how to teach themselves, go beyond the lessons available and learn the skills they need to go further.

It Takes a Micro Computer Village

Have you heard of the Raspberry Pi? It's a tiny single-board computer (**SBC**) about the size of a credit card, and about the price of a couple of pizzas. It's not a wimpy little thing, either: the P1 2 has a quad-core CPU, USB and HDMI video. A tiny microSD card serves as the hard drive, and swaps so easily you can use several operating systems.

Figure 1.4: *a Raspberry Pi*

The Raspberry Pi isn't the only microcomputer out there. Other manufacturers sell the Banana Pi, the Orange Pi, the BeagleBone, the Radxa Rock – each with a unique set of features. Want built-in Bluetooth and wifi, for instance? One of the above offers exactly that. (Start researching.)

There are basically three types of microcomputers; the first is the Linux-based board that can act as a full computer or server. The next is an Arduino device that is more of a controller for sensors, robotic equipment, lighting control and basic items. The last type of microcomputer is the hybrid device that is built for specific purposes like controlling sensors but can also be a computer to a point.

The Raspberry Pi (RPi) is in the first category since it runs Linux. This computer has a 1GHZ Cortex Arm quad core processor with 1 gig of ram. The board includes a GPU, four USB ports, an ethernet port, HDMI video output, audio output and a 40-pin GPIO connector to add additional parts onto it. (The attachments have a fun name: because they are Hardware Attached on Top, they're called "HATs" - but that's only with Pies.) You can find them for well under $50, even lower for older models.

Figure 1.5: *Bob Monroe displaying a varied collection at Micro Computer Village*

You can learn programming (python, scratch, java, php and others) on this device. It can also be used as a server for email, web, multimedia, VPN, or even a NAT firewall. One very popular use is as a Minecraft server. There is a huge collection of information available on the Internet for this device.

Arduino devices are made in Italy and were primarily built to teach coding, control sensors and robotic equipment. These devices are a bit more expensive and are more customized for specific jobs. These require some expertise to work with.

Hybrid devices include Udoo, Remix, Radxa Rock and others. The prices for these vary greatly but often include wifi and Bluetooth built in. Neither Arduino nor Raspberry Pi have these connections but it doesn't cost much to add them on (except the Arduino Yun which has wifi built in). The hybrids are built to act as controllers and computers on a much higher level than the RPi or Arduino. The Remix is a full blown computer that runs a special version of Android. The Udoo tries to replace the RPi and Arduino with a single device.

Figure 1.6: *The Udoo Neo*

If you are looking to start out, we would suggest the RPi as your first step. It is cheap but requires a learning curve to set working. All of these devices use a microSD card to hold the operating system. Luckily, most devices allow you to choose which operating system you want to work with. Changing operating systems is as simple as swapping out the microSD card.

Figure 1.7: Programming a *Raspberry Pi*

Most of the devices connect to a TV or monitor using HDMI. You can connect a wireless or USB keyboard to control your device or puTTY in based on the local IP address of the device.

Keep Going!

Now you should practice until you're a master of researching. The better you get at it, the more information you will find quickly, and the faster you will learn. But be careful also to develop a critical eye. Not all information is truth.

> Always remember to ask yourself, why would someone lie? Is there money involved in being dishonest or perpetuating a rumor or story? Where do the facts come from? And most importantly, what is the scope?

Like all hacking, research includes a scope. That's really important when you see statistics, like math that uses percentages and fractions and odds. Always look to see where the scope took place and recognize that the scope has to apply. A common place you see this is national crime or health statistics taken from a small sample in just one part of the country. Just because something affects 10% of people out of 200 studied in a single city doesn't mean that 10% of the whole nation has this same problem. So be smart about how you read information as well as how you find it. Figuring out the scope of the information always makes a huge difference!

To help you become a better researcher for the Hacker Highschool program, here are some additional topics and terms for you to investigate:

- Meta Search
- The Invisible Web
- The Dark Web
- Google Hacking
- How Search Engines Work
- The Hacker Jargon File
- OSSTMM

Hacking Email

Introduction to Hacking Email

Email has been around for a long time; like longer than those socks stuffed under your bed. It predates the Internet (not your dirty socks), and is one of the first forms of electronic information exchange. Before email, we had smoke signals, half-naked guys running as messengers, bricks with notes attached, Morse code, large rocks slung over castle walls with curse words written on them, and a variety of other analog communication methods like the telephone and paper "snail mail" (not really delivered by snails). Many of these original message transmission required special tools, training, or lots of rocks. Luckily, enterprising authors created text that could be written on stone tablets or bound in books and thrown at people or read by them. One of the first books was *Smoke Signals for Dummies*.

Email is based on simple store and forward principles. It can be relatively easy to use (unless you are in a huge hurry), very robust and so cheap that it is often abused for commercial and criminal purposes. Its asynchronous design allows communication to take place without the need for sender and receiver to both be online at the same time. Kind of like when your mother is talking to you and you're not paying attention until she asks you a question. You are not there for the transmission but you better be a quick deceiver. Um, receiver. A quick receiver.

In this lesson, we will focus on modern Internet email and hacking or security issues you can use for fun and profit.

How Email Works

First, we are going to pretend that you are an email. You will follow the transmission and receipt of yourself as an email, and we will identify the various components that move you along.

1. Email (you) is (are) created either using an email **client** or a web-based email service through a web browser. It's almost funny how much email mimics "snail mail," because your message is enclosed in an envelope, like in Figure 2.1.

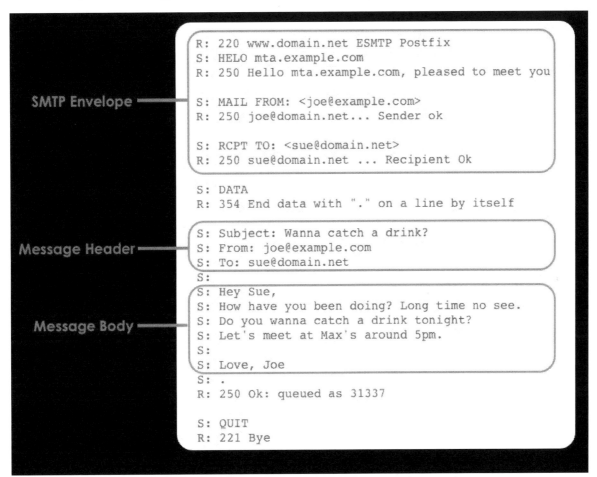

Figure 2.1: Email message, headers and envelope

2. You are sent to a mail server called a **Mail Transmission Agent (MTA)**, which queues you for transmission. Modern mail systems do this typically via encrypted **SMTP (Simple Mail Transport Protocol)** since they require authentication to prevent abuse, and encryption protects credentials from disclosure, along with the email contents. MTAs accepting email (you) without some sort of authentication are called "open

relays" and tend to be abused by senders of junk mail, also known as UCE (Unsolicited Commercial Email) or **spam**.

3. For each address ("recipient") in the message, the MTA first checks if a recipient is local (right on the same computer). If not, the MTA uses a so-called MX record (explained below) to find the server for the relevant domain. If there is no valid receiving host found, a failure message for that specific address is sent back to the sender.

4. The MTA attempts to deliver you to each address. If this fails, the MTA re-queues the message to try again later until timeout occurs and a delivery failure message is returned, usually in 48 hours. So you have to hang around for about two days. This delivery may initially be deliberately delayed by the receiving MTA as an anti-spam technique: spam software is typically less intelligent and will not queue and retry delivery (the technique is called **greylisting**). By default, this delivery takes place via **unencrypted** SMTP. Encrypted connections are the exception rather than the rule.

5. Optionally, a mail relay picks you up and routes you to your final destination. This typically happens in environments with spam and virus filtering and where security dictates a layered model, such as enterprise or government networks.

Did you catch that reference to a **layered security model**? Those heavy-duty government security guys can't create M&Ms, hard on the outside but soft in the middle. They put in lots of layers of armor: router controls and firewalls, intrusion detection systems (IDS), anti-virus, anti-malware, spam control and a whole lot more.

Which sounds pretty tough to hack. But never forget: every program you install adds more code, with more vulnerabilities, and the same goes for hardware. That cool VPN device, for instance, might give you "secure" VPN – or it might offer backdoors of its own. It depends a lot on whether you're Red Team or Blue Team how much you like this.

6. The receiving MTA expands the address if it is an alias or a mailing list. These do not need to be in the same domain: an alias can expand into a whole new email address on another server. After expansion, you are re-queued for further delivery.

7. When an email address refers to a local mailbox, you are now moved into that mailbox (unless the mailbox has exceeded its storage quota). You might be too big. You gotta stop eating so much junk food.

8. You are then picked up via the POP3 or IMAP protocol by webmail or a mail client. Here too, the connection is generally encrypted (with SSL) to prevent leaking login credentials; the protocols are POP3S and SSL IMAP. POP3 is a "pick up" process: it downloads messages, then deletes them from the server (this can be date driven). IMAP is a synchronization process that seeks to keep clients' mailboxes identical to what is on the server account (for mobile devices this is typically within a date range to preserve device storage), which makes IMAP perfect to maintain email on multiple devices at the same time.

9. Finally, most email clients now have junk mail detection built in, usually based on Bayesian, pattern scoring principles. Try sending your friend an email with "Viagra" in the Subject to see how this works.

The Three Stages of Spam Filtering

1. Receiving servers first check on origin: an SMTP connection is refused from blacklisted servers (various companies exist to provide these lists).

2. When a connection is accepted, email is then scanned for content. Some organizations are concerned they may have a message falsely marked as junk mail; they may require suspect email to be marked as junk, but still delivered.

3. Finally, most email clients now have junk mail detection built in, usually based on Bayesian, pattern-scoring principles.

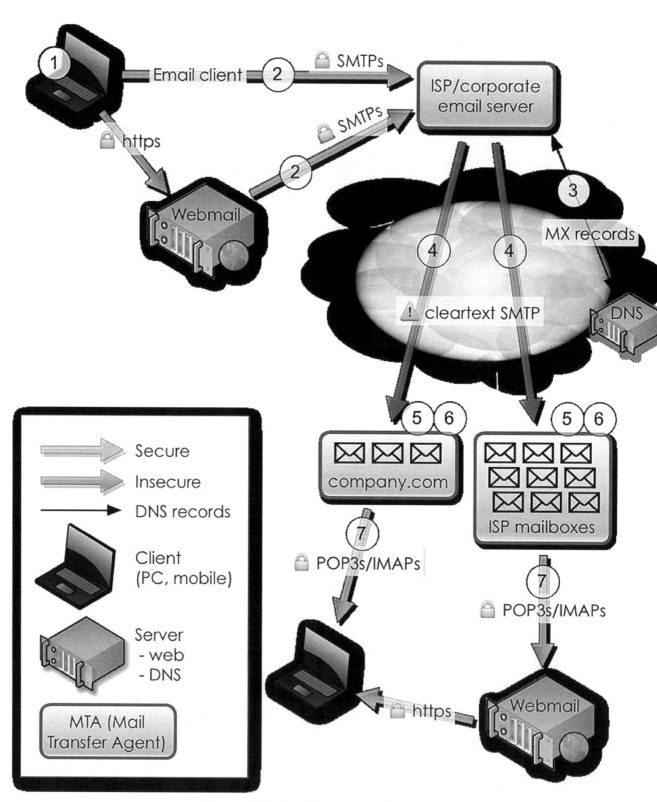

Figure 2.2: *Email process flow*

So, there ya go. That was easy, wasn't it? You start at one place and may or may not end up at another place, depending on whether:

- You have the correct address

- You are spam

- You are too big

- The receiving mail box is too small

- or you are too old.

With all this great information you now know how emails move through the digital world. Everything you need to know about life can come from email traffic.

- Know where you are going.

- Don't eat spam.

- Get big mail boxes (communicate a lot).

- Don't get big (Eat right and exercise to maintain a healthy lifestyle).

- Lastly, don't get old.

See how easy that is?

Feed Your Head: Email Headers

A **message**, from the SMTP point of view, consists of **headers** and a **body**. Headers are machine-parseable statements containing information of all kinds, the most basic ones being headers like 'To:' for the mail recipient or 'Subject:'. The sender address might be quickly dismissed as a basic piece of information easy to describe but we'll see that it's a more complex concept.

The body of the message contains everything else (everything other than headers) and it's not normally supposed to be parsed by MTAs (although, as we'll see, it might happen for filtering purposes). Usually the body of the message contains simple text but it can also be HTML (which often annoys really technical people), and in multi-part messages (i.e. messages with attachments) MIME is used. MIME stands for Multipurpose Internet Mail Extensions and it's a standard that is used for sending character encodings other than plain ASCII and binary content. MIME is automatically used by the email client when needed.

Some headers can be removed, some can be modified and some will be added by different components in the mail flow process. Every MTA should always add a "Received" header for tracking its role the email path during transmission. In theory, by looking at the headers you should always be able to track the original sender. We'll soon see why this is not always the case.

There's a set of headers that every email should have in order to be parseable by the SMTP standard, some headers that most SMTP implementations consider standard but that really are not, and some custom headers (X-*) that are customizable and can contain any sort of message. Think of it as a way to shift user-definable content from the body to the headers. Some of the most widely used examples are filtering applications information (X-Spam) and MUA (X-Mailer). (It's not uncommon to spot very interesting customized headers in the wild; email from security consultants may have weird ones!)

Consider this example.

```
[Sample message]

From root@isecom.org Sat Sep 30 13:50:39 2006
Return-Path: <root@isecom.org>
Received: from isecom.org (localhost.localdomain [127.0.0.1])
     by isecom.org (8.13.8/8.13.7) with ESMTP id k8UBodHB001194
     for <test@isecom.org>; Sat, 30 Sep 2006 13:50:39 +0200
Received: (from root@localhost)
     by isecom.org (8.13.8/8.13.5/Submit) id k8UBoNcZ001193
     for root; Sat, 30 Sep 2006 13:50:23 +0200
Date: Sat, 30 Sep 2006 13:50:23 +0200
Message-Id: <200609301150.k8UBoNcZ001193@isecom.org>
From: root@isecom.org
To: test@isecom.org
Subject: foobar

test
```

If you look at your raw mailbox, you can sometimes see an additional "From" followed by a space and then a sender address, without the colon seen in the usual "From:" header. That's an internal separator for messages defined by the mbox storage format and it's not really an SMTP header.

The **Mail Delivery Agent (MDA)**, which is the component responsible for storing the message in final delivery, also has the task of protecting any existing line that begins with "From" in the body of the message, a process that's prone to misinterpretation.

The sample message shown above was transmitted with the following SMTP transaction:

```
CONNECT [127.0.0.1]
220 isecom.org ESMTP Sendmail 8.13.8/8.13.7; Sat, 30 Sep 2006 14:08:38
+0200
EHLO isecom.org
250-isecom.org Hello localhost.localdomain [127.0.0.1], pleased to meet
you
250-ENHANCEDSTATUSCODES
250-PIPELINING
250-8BITMIME
250-SIZE 5000000
250-DSN
250-ETRN
250-DELIVERBY
250 HELP
MAIL From:<root@isecom.org> SIZE=57
250 2.1.0 <root@isecom.org>... Sender ok
RCPT To:<test@isecom.org>
DATA
250 2.1.5 <test@isecom.org>... Recipient ok
Received: (from root@localhost)
        by isecom.org (8.13.8/8.13.5/Submit) id k8UC8EMj001346
        for root; Sat, 30 Sep 2006 14:08:14 +0200
Date: Sat, 30 Sep 2006 14:08:14 +0200
Message-Id: <200609301208.k8UC8EMj001346@isecom.org>
From: root@isecom.org
To: test@isecom.org
Subject: foobar

test
.
250 2.0.0 k8UC8c3M001347 Message accepted for delivery
QUIT
221 2.0.0 isecom.org closing connection
```

The path of an email message is traced with the "Received" headers:

```
Delivered-To: <spoofer@isecom.org>
Return-Path: test@isecom.org
Received: from smtp.isecom.org (smtp.isecom.org [140.211.166.183])
        by azzurra.isecom.org (8.13.6/8.13.6) with ESMTP id
```

```
    k4KL5UOq014773
            (version=TLSv1/SSLv3 cipher=DHE-RSA-AES256-SHA bits=256
verify=NO)
            for <spoofer@isecom.org>; Sat, 20 May 2006 21:05:30 GMT
Received: by smtp.isecom.org (Postfix)
            id D138A64413; Sat, 20 May 2006 21:05:29 +0000 (UTC)
Delivered-To: spoofer@isecom.org
Received: from localhost (localhost [127.0.0.1])
            by smtp.isecom.org (Postfix) with ESMTP id B87EF64409
            for <spoofer@isecom.org>; Sat, 20 May 2006 21:05:29 +0000 (UTC)
Received: from smtp.isecom.org ([127.0.0.1])
  by localhost (smtp.isecom.org [127.0.0.1]) (amavisd-new, port 10024)
 with ESMTP id 24780-13 for <spoofer@isecom.org>;
 Sat, 20 May 2006 21:05:23 +0000 (UTC)
Received: from mail2.isecom.org (bsiC.pl [83.18.69.210])
            (using TLSv1 with cipher DHE-RSA-AES256-SHA (256/256 bits))
            (No client certificate requested)
            by smtp.isecom.org (Postfix) with ESMTP id 6B37E64405
            for <spoofer@isecom.org>; Sat, 20 May 2006 21:05:23 +0000 (UTC)
Received: from localhost (localhost.isecom.org [127.0.0.1])
            by mail2.isecom.org (Postfix) with ESMTP id BDF11B02DE
            for <spoofer@isecom.org>; Sat, 20 May 2006 23:12:55 +0200 (CEST)
Received: from mail2.isecom.org ([127.0.0.1])
  by localhost ([127.0.0.1]) (amavisd-new, port 10024) with ESMTP
  id 11508-04 for <spoofer@isecom.org>; Sat, 20 May 2006 23:12:42 +0200
(CEST)
Received: from localhost (unknown [192.168.0.5])
            by mail2.isecom.org (Postfix) with ESMTP id 54666B02DC
            for <spoofer@isecom.org>; Sat, 20 May 2006 23:12:41 +0200 (CEST)
Date: Sat, 20 May 2006 23:05:04 +0200
From: John Doe <test@isecom.org>
To: spoofer@isecom.org
```

The way to read these headers is backwards. You start with the last as the point of origin and read up to the destination. Now check out some of the headers from mails you've received.

Dig Me

When you're working in Linux and UNIX in general, **dig** is your best friend for testing DNS settings. MX records are very important to email delivery, so let's have a look at them briefly. MX records are for email, and have no relationship to websites for the same domain. The web server of "domain.com" may be a completely different system from the mail server, which is why those DNS records are identified differently.

The way to get MX records is by using the dig command from a UNIX, Linux, or OSX command line. dig is a DNS information tool, and as any UNIX program it has a gazillion options. We will just use one format. Using

```
dig <domain name> MX
```

tells dig to extract only mail exchange records from the relevant domain. Another easy example is

```
dig <servername> <type>
```

For example the public DNS server 213.133.105.2 ns.second-ns.de can be used for testing. See which server the client receives the answer.

```
dig sleepyowl.net
sleepyowl.net.          600     IN      A       78.31.70.238
;; SERVER: 192.168.51.254#53(192.168.51.254)
```

The local router 192.168.51.254 answered and the response is the A entry. Any entry can be queried and the DNS server can be selected with @:

```
dig MX google.com                      # Get the mail MX entry
dig @127.0.0.1 NS sun.com              # To test the local server
dig @204.97.212.10 NS MX heise.de      # Query an external server
dig AXFR @ns1.xname.org cb.vu          # Get the full zone (zone transfer)
```

The command host is also powerful.

```
host -t MX cb.vu                       # Get the mail MX entry
host -t NS -T sun.com                  # Get the NS record
host -a sleepyowl.net                  # Get everything
```

As a larger example, here are the MX records for Google's *gmail.com* domain:

```
;; ANSWER SECTION:
gmail.com.          893     IN      MX      10 alt1.gmail-smtp-in.l.google.com.
gmail.com.          893     IN      MX      40 alt4.gmail-smtp-in.l.google.com.
gmail.com.          893     IN      MX      30 alt3.gmail-smtp-in.l.google.com.
gmail.com.          893     IN      MX      20 alt2.gmail-smtp-in.l.google.com.
gmail.com.          893     IN      MX      5 gmail-smtp-in-v4v6.l.google.com.
```

There are three values in each line that are of interest. The "893" is a **time to live** value (how many seconds, or how many routers to hop, depending) you will find in every DNS record – it indicates how long a DNS is allowed to cache the record before the information is considered stale and has to be retrieved again.

The "10" in the top line, and "40", "30", "20" and "5" in subsequent lines are "preference" values, followed by a **Fully Qualified Domain Name (FQDN)** of a system prepared to handle email. The preference values are used by the MTA to decide which of the machines in the MX records list to try first, and which to contact next, should the first one fail or refuse email. If no server is found to accept the email, a failure message is sent back to the email originator (using the "reply-to" or "from" information). Lower values indicate preferred MTAs. Thus, the last entry in the list above will be tried first, with the rest as fallback if the first system fails or is overloaded.

A service can also offer records with identical preferences; here is the response from yahoo.com where the preferences value is set to "1" on all records:

```
;; ANSWER SECTION:

yahoo.com.          48    IN    MX    1 mta6.am0.yahoodns.net.

yahoo.com.          48    IN    MX    1 mta5.am0.yahoodns.net.

yahoo.com.          48    IN    MX    1 mta7.am0.yahoodns.net.
```

Doing this means the email load will be distributed over the 3 systems equally. The very low TTL value of "48" suggests this DNS entry is dynamically controlled, a sign of an active load balancer. Load balancers do pretty much what their name says they do; they make sure traffic (inbound, outbound, high priority, low priority) gets the level of attention it deserves.

Last but not least, you can also identify whether the receiving domain uses mail filtering. The famous domain no10.gsi.gov.uk (the domain of Britain's Prime Minister) shows that a company called MessageLabs is presently responsible for mail filtering:

```
;; ANSWER SECTION:

no10.gsi.gov.uk. 3600  IN    MX    20 cluster.gsi2.messagelabs.com.

no10.gsi.gov.uk. 3600  IN    MX    10 cluster.gsi.messagelabs.com.
```

You do not need to fear black helicopters when you look this up: this information is public, as email would otherwise not work. Besides, the UK military only has *green* helicopters!

Exercises

2.1 Does your email platform support a "Delivery Receipt" or any kind of delivery flag that lets you know (at least) that your mail reached some destination? If it does exchange messages with a friend and examine the headers from that traffic.

2.2 Choose a domain name. Find out which system handles email for that domain by looking up MX records.

Game On: The Bug Trap

The cafeteria floor was slightly damp, almost like fly paper, with a stickiness pulling at the bottom of her rubber soled shoes. Jace glanced at the reflective sheen of the gunk floor wondering how a place that serves food could smell so bad but keep a mirror shine. The odor reminded her of when her Grandpa used to place the cockroach traps behind the apartment couch. As Grandpa pulled out the old trap, Jace could see the encrusted remains. It seemed like the entire inside of the roach trap was filled with dead bugs.

She was never shy about asking questions. "Why don't the roaches just leave the box? Can't they see all their friends in there dead?" she asked Grandpa more than once just to be sure she got the right answer each time. Jace loved to watch Grandpa work, often getting in the way by putting her head right over his shoulder. He never complained. He always loved having his granddaughter right by his side as much as possible.

"Jace, the roaches are attracted to this trap by the smell inside the box. As soon as they go inside the trap, the floor is really sticky and they get stuck in the box. It's like they are glued to the floor. They don't seem to notice all the other dead insects inside and they die too," her grandfather would explain in roughly the same version each time he was asked.

"Roaches aren't very smart," little Jace would reply with a smug smile.

"Yes, my dear, you are much smarter than a cockroach."

"Thank you, I guess."

Back at the school cafeteria, coffee brown hair fell into her face as she continued to look at the mirror floor; she needed to get back her classwork.

Just out the corner of her right eye, Jace caught a sudden commotion at the cafeteria double doors. They swung open as several people burst into the large open room. Instantly going into clandestine mode, she leaned forward and let her thin shoulder-length hair cover her face. She heard, "There, she's over there trying to hide herself! Grab Jace. Don't let her move!" Several older voices shrilled with the excitement of a witch hunt.

The teen hacker held her position at the table, clenching her knapsack and pretending to be unaware of the coming attack. Knives, pitchforks, torches, angry mobs and all those monster movie images compressed themselves into her calculating mind. Curiosity got the best of her and she looked up to see the school principal, his secretary, Mr. Tri, three freshmen table tennis players and several other oddballs approaching. The roar of their voices was tremendous as it bounced against the polished floor towards her.

"Hold on! I said hold on," a familiar voice commanded somewhere behind the angry freaks. The mob lost momentum. The freshmen parted the crowd so the Chief of Police could step through the cluster of confusion. "Alright folks, thank you for your overzealous help locating Ms. Jace for me. Now, I would like to have a moment alone with her," the chief said in a calming voice. He'd used that same voice to talk down a jumper off a 14 story building years ago. It worked then, it sort of worked now. The crowd became a loose net of individuals trying to look busy, tying their shoelaces, too obviously stretching to listen to the chief's private conversation.

"Hi Jace," Chief couldn't think of anything else to open with.

"Yes, Police Chief. How may I help you at MY school, while I am enjoying MY lunch. With MY peers all staring at ME," she almost broke her jaw clenching her teeth.

"I apologize. I'm sorry to interrupt your massive gathering of friends here but I need your help now," the chief said, trying to keep his cool, but also letting Jace know that this wasn't the time to be difficult. Jace unclenched her hands from her pack and looked the Chief in the face. He tilted his head towards the double cafeteria doors, motioning her to follow him.

Jace looked down at her unfinished sandwich, reluctant. The Chief didn't take his eyes off of her. He raised his right hand and slapped his fingers in the air. Jace flinched. The entire lunchroom flinched. Principal Mantral realized what the signal meant and came rushing forward with a clear plastic bag.

"Cookies, eh," Jace asked.

"Chocolate chip pecan, made by Officer Hank's wife," Chief replied. "Deal?"

"Deal," she replied with one cookie already in her mouth.

As the two walked out of the school, the chief asked if Jace had ever ridden in a SWAT van before. "That was the only vehicle I could get at the last minute. Sorry," he said. The two of them left the school looking like rock stars in the SWAT van. Jace laughed looking in the rearview mirror at the stunned students and school staff.

"Here's what is going on. Someone is looking at my email. I don't know how or who or why but I do know that my emails are being hacked. I need you to help me stop this. It's causing major problems with our law enforcement capabilities," the Chief didn't give Jace a chance to interrupt. "When you set up our network last summer, you did a bunch of extra security stuff. It hasn't been enough. I can tell you that one email three weeks ago concerned a technicality on a particular suspect we had. Only me and the District Attorney knew about this problem."

The police chief reached across the van console to grab a cookie from the open bag. Jace jokingly slapped his hand away. He reached down towards his baton that he didn't wear since he was a wasn't a street cop anymore. Jace relented and handed him a large pecan piece to keep him talking, which he did, cookie crumbs littering his uniform.

"Two hours after the DA and I emailed each other, I get a call from the front desk telling me that the suspect just posted bail. The suspect's lawyer found out about the technicality and got a judge to sign off on release for the suspect. There were only two people who knew about this technicality and that was through my email," the Chief said.

He continued, "Last week I got a call about the possibility of some missing evidence at a crime scene. That was just an anonymous phone call. There wasn't any specific item mentioned in that call. I wrote a quick email to our evidence clerk asking for the inventory log for the entire weeks' worth of cases, especially the log from that day. The clerk emails me the log and I compare it to the police report from the crime. Being the thorough investigator I am, I delete all the information in the log file that isn't relevant and forwarded the log file to our Internal Investigation team."

Jace is trying to understand what he is saying in-between all his police jargon. "So?" she blurted out, feeling much better after her sandwich and five cookies.

The chief looked a bit annoyed but answered anyway, "So! So there isn't any missing evidence that we can tell. Later that day, I get another call from the DA asking me where the murder weapon is from that same case. It didn't occur to me that the gun was missing from the evidence locker. Again, two hours later another suspect is out on bail because the police and forensic team didn't document or turn in the pistol used in the crime."

Jace, wishing she had a large cold glass of milk, chimed in, "So the mysterious caller was checking to see if the gun has in police custody. The email you sent to your Internal Thugs, verified that the weapon was never entered in as police evidence."

The police chief had an amazing smile of satisfaction when she finished her conclusion. "Ya know, Jace, you'd make a terrific police detective when you get older."

Jace shot back, "Yeah, well, I have too much self-respect to be a cop. I'd rather be a lawyer or a politician or some other lower form of life." Luckily she started to giggle as she said the last part because the chief was getting angry with her insult. "Just joking, Chief."

Game continues...

The Risky Business of Email Composition

- **Disclosure**. Think about whom you are emailing, why and how. Not only is email transmission by default insecure when it leaves the local MTA, you are also releasing information. The use of encryption such as PGP, GPG and S/MIME requires both sides to be similarly equipped, and is generally perceived as very complicated to use (translated: users avoid it with enthusiasm). An alternative way to protect the transmission would be the use of the *same* email provider: that way, the message never needs to travel across the Internet in an unencrypted form. This is where the *how* question appears: are you sure your provider or that of the recipient (or one or the other of your governments) is not listening in? Take that into consideration when you handle something confidential.

- **Rerouting**. An email address does not need to remain in the domain it is sent to, but could be redirected elsewhere. As an example, the US company *pobox.com* does not sell mailbox services, only aliases. The main risk is that your email may thus travel over various, different legal jurisdictions before it arrives at its destination. In our example, a *pobox.com* alias will always go via MTAs in the US first, and is thus at risk of interception under the ongoing abuse of the US PATRIOT Act.

- **Privacy violations**. A recipient using services such as Facebook or Google exposes his email to automated scanning of content, even though the *sender* never gave that permission!

- **Distribution lists**. If you use an email distribution list, use the BCC (blind carbon copy) field for it. Email addresses in the TO: and CC: field are visible to every recipient of the email, and could end up giving away the contents of your email list to an uncontrolled third party, and expose your recipients to spam and other junk mail.

- **Conflict**. An email is like a letter, but is written and sent much more quickly, which leaves you less time to consider its contents. Writing email is like driving: it's best not done in anger. In case of emotional involvement, write a draft and leave it for an hour, then reconsider if you really should send it. It could save a friendship or a career.

- **Misaddressing**. One of the main causes of email going astray is misaddressing. This is a consequence of mail clients trying to autofill an address from the characters typed by the user. Always check if the recipient is indeed the intended one.

- **Multiple recipients**. When you send email to more than one person, make sure the content is appropriate for all recipients. Also, it is good practice and ethically correct to visibly copy someone in if you use their information or talk about them.

- **Legal issues**. Disclaimers under your email may look impressive, but have no legal value other than a copyright notice. You sent the email, so you cannot disavow its content (to a degree, of course you could always claim its sender was spoofed) and you cannot prescribe what an incorrect recipient should do with an email because you probably don't have a contractual relation with them. (See the Ultimate Disclaimer at the end of this lesson.)

- **Top posting.** When you reply to an email, does your email program automatically put your reply on top of the original message? This seems to be the default these days, but unfortunately it's … rude. Recipients who have to start from your reply and work their way down to some context aren't likely to love you. On the other hand, weren't they in on the original message to begin with? Consider, at least, whether you want to engage in "top posting."

- **Autoresponders.** "You sent me an email so I'm sending you this automatic email response to let you know I won't get your email until I return, so heaven help us both if you've got an autoresponder too, because this is going to go in circles until the end of the universe." This stuff can drive you crazy, but it's also an awfully convenient notice to evildoers that you're probably not at home. What was your street address again?

- **Signatures.** Do you use a signature, an automatic "Yours Truly, Stardonk Cluck, Program Manager for Automated Actions" that sticks itself to the bottom of every message you send? They're not necessarily bad – until they get really long. And ten of them stack up at the bottom of a long back-and-forth conversation. And they are all in HTML, not polite plain text, so that your graphic of a gorilla climbing a skyscraper appears over and over and over. Be kind about using a signature, and don't subject your recipient to the dangers of HTML email at all if you can help it.

Exercises

2.3 Head over to http://www.gaijin.at/en/olsmailheader.php and insert an email header you've taken from any email. This program is an analyzer that will provide you information about that email header. From the information given, what can you do with these results?

Receiving Email

Mail clients contact the servers on which mailboxes are stored, and check if the top message count has not changed. Some clients do this periodically (for instance, every 30 minutes), some do it manually (usually to preserve bandwidth) and some maintain a simple permanent connection with the mail server so that they receive an update as soon as new email arrives (called **push notification**).

When an email is inbound, the mail client or webmail environment will pick this up via POP3 or IMAP. Mobile clients usually download only the header and a small portion of the message to save bandwidth, leaving it up to the user to decide if the whole message should be picked up, left for later or deleted.

The early days of email communication took place over unreliable, slow connections, and the handling of attachment such as documents, spreadsheets or images still shows this. An attachment must always be downloaded in full before it can be displayed. Users using webmail on a third party computer such as in cyber cafes must be careful: **viewing an attachment means leaving a copy behind on the system's hard disk**. By default, those are **not** erased after use.

Webmail on an untrusted computer naturally carries another risk: unless you use one-time passwords, you may leave behind your email access credentials because there is no guarantee the third party machine is not infected or monitored.

Systems with active email should have up-to-date antivirus protection, but you should understand that antivirus only protects against **known** malware. Especially with targeted attacks, it can take several days before malware is added to virus scanners; some malware is never added at all.

Incoming email contains a travel history in the headers. Every system mail passes through adds a line in the hidden part of the header, with the latest one on top. However, be aware this is also easy to forge: keep in mind that not all entries may be real.

Exercise

2.4 Consider the "temporary" files people leave behind when they use email. You can see a lot by looking into temp directories (there are usually more than one). Windows, for instance, makes it easy to see what's in temp directories even if you don't know where they are: the **%temp%** variable knows all of them.

Open a command-line interface in Windows and type

```
dir %temp%
```

What do you see?

For an even handier view, use Windows Explorer by typing this command:

```
explorer %temp%
```

2.5 Open up the email header on any email. See if you can locate any additional receivers besides you. They might be located in the carbon copy (cc) section of the email header.

- Select several emails. Check the mail path and origin via mail headers. Check what other information is available in the headers (hint: email client and antivirus software versions; encryption algorithms; etc.).

- Compare the sender and reply-to addresses

- Have a look at some junk mail. What do you see in those headers compared to normal emails? Check where all the links go (just as text, not by going there). Do the links URLs go where the text says they are going?

Responding to Email

Responding to email needs to be done with some care. How many times have you said something or done something that you didn't mean or wish you could take back?

First of all, NEVER react to what is clearly junk mail, even if it is to unsubscribe. All you do is confirm that (a) the email account is live and (b) someone at that email address actually reads junk mail. The result of the cancellation attempt is thus, ironically, *more* junk mail.

Check for address disclosure. Do all recipients need to be visible? If you use a mailing list, are all recipients still valid? Does every recipient really need to see your answer?

Be hygienic. Does the whole email need to be repeated or can you just use the parts that are relevant? If you re-use parts of a previous email you can show that by "quoting" - a way to make it visible you are repeating part of an email, and then respond to that specific part.

Be careful with quoting: is all that you repeat actually meant for the recipients you are selecting now, or are you including (parts of) a discussion that was confidential and not meant for the new recipient(s)? Avoid quoting the whole original message including signature and (usually extensive) disclaimer. Be aware that whatever you send can be forwarded on to anyone without your permission or knowledge too. It is a good and polite habit to copy a person in when you talk about them or refer to something they have done, so they know what has being said about them, and it prompts you to avoid stating something you may regret later. Delivery flags are helpful in keeping an eye on email as it travels to its destination, and by looking up MX records you can work out where the email will go. You could use geolocation to give you a physical location as well. Delivery flags also chew up bandwidth. Because a delivery flag was set, your email server must send a response. Not everyone appreciates emails flagged as "urgent" or "important." Flags such as these are usually an indicator that the message is spam, if they weren't sent by a co-worker.

Exercises

2.6 Forward an email to another account and compare headers.

- How can headers be used against you, and how you could prevent this from happening?

- Can you forward an email that was sent to you as a blind copy (BCC)?

2.7 Write yourself an email and send it to yourself. During delivery, quickly retract that email (unsend). If the email was successfully pulled back, take a look at the header of that draft email. Copy that header to a text editor and see if you can locate which email server stopped that email from going through. Cool huh?

Cryptography Protecting Contents From Disclosure

The simplicity of email makes it also vulnerable. The sender cannot be sure that an email is not altered on its way to the recipient, there is no way to make sure that only the receiver can read it and a receiver cannot be sure it is actually sent by the person listed in the email as the sender.

One way to ensure confidentiality is to encrypt a document before attaching it to an email. For example, it is possible to encrypt text documents and spreadsheets like those produced by OpenOffice, and PDF files support encryption too. However, applying cryptography to email itself is easier, and also allows for the email contents to be secured.

Email headers still need to be left in cleartext so that the mail servers can process and deliver the email.

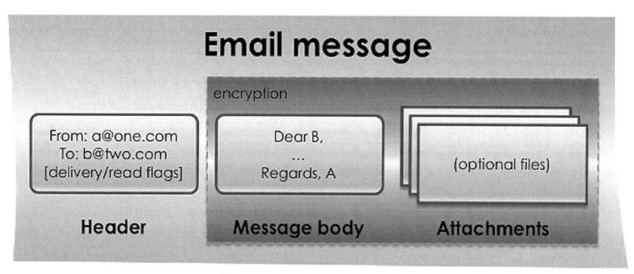

Figure 2.3: *Email encryption*

Email security can be provided in two different ways: using PGP (or GPG) and S/MIME. Both use encryption to assure:

- **C**onfidentiality: can only the intended recipient(s) read this email?

- **I**ntegrity: is the email content unchanged?

- **A**uthenticity: did the email really come from a particular sender?

(An easy way to remember this list is the acronym they form: **CIA**.)

In general, authenticity and integrity are combined in electronically **signing** an email: the email gets checksummed, and the result is encrypted and embedded in an electronic signature that could only have been made by the person who holds the right private key (see "PGP and GPG" below).

Confidentiality is assured by using someone's public key to encrypt the message body, so that only the holder of the correct private key can decrypt and read it (see "PGP and GPG" below). For extra assurance, such a message can be signed too.

You should keep in mind that encrypted email is rather uncommon, especially in an era where people voluntarily let their email be scanned by companies such as Google and Facebook. In some countries, you must make sure that you have the means to access your email when authorities demand this of you, for instance in the US by the TSA when you cross the border, and in the UK when served with a warrant under the Regulation of Investigative Powers Act.

PGP and GPG

PGP stands for Pretty Good Privacy and was developed by Phil Zimmermann. The history of PGP is interesting and certainly worth reading, but for the purposes of this chapter we will only focus on its use.

You are more likely to come across the Open Source version called GPG (GNU Privacy Guard). GPG is available for free for many platforms, and only uses open, publicly evaluated algorithms.

GPG works on the principle of **public/private key management**, which means that keys have a PUBLIC part you can give to anyone who wants to send you encrypted email, and a PRIVATE part you have to keep secret, which is the only way to decipher the message you have received. The combination of private and public key is called a **key pair**, and it is generally the first thing you generate when you install GPG on a machine. The key pair is protected by a password so that it cannot be altered by anyone but the owner. Alterations may be necessary because you want to change the email addresses the key supports, or want to make use of other functions.

Because you need someone's public key to encrypt a message to them, servers such as pgp.mit.edu exist where you can download the key or keys associated with a specific email address and upload your own. It is possible that keys have expired or passwords have been lost, so always use the latest key or even better, ask your recipient to send theirs and confirm the key fingerprint (a short version of the checksum).

MIME Your Manners

MIME (Multi-Purpose Internet Mail Extensions) is an email extension of the Simple Mail Transfer Protocol (SMTP). MIME gives you the ability to transfer different types of media and data like audio, video, images, compressed files, and applications as attachments to email. The MIME header is inserted at the beginning of the email and the receiving email client uses this information to determine which program is associated with the attached file. MIME in itself does not provide any security to emails or attachments.

S/MIME (Secure/Multipurpose Internet Mail Extensions) is a protocol that adds digital signatures and encryption to Internet MIME message attachments. Using digital signatures, S/MIME allows for authentication, message integrity and **non-repudiation** of origin ("non-repudiation" means you can't deny you sent it). S/MIME provides privacy and data security (using encryption) to emails that use this protocol.

S/MIME is both a security tool and a security issue since users can send sensitive data or secrets as attachments to outbound emails in order to avoid detection. Therefore, the use of S/MIME in a corporate setting should be carefully monitored on the email servers.

Key Trust

How do you ensure that a key for an email recipient is really theirs, and not uploaded by someone else? The solution to this is that keys can be signed by others. Imagine you already have the key of someone else who you trust, and who knows the person you want to email with. That other person can **sign** the public key, which means you invest a bit more trust in the key, provided you know this other person. This is known as **inherited trust**. You can also find another way to get in touch with the person and either receive their full public key, or receive the key "fingerprint" - a checksum of the key which is quick to verify. On a key server, a key can also have an ID – yet another checksum serving the same goal.

Feed Your Head: Is The Web Of Trust Model Valid?

From research done by ISECOM, we know the **Web of Trust** model used by PGP/GPG, unfortunately, isn't actually valid. One simple example illustrates why: if you trust your friend, and your friend trusts his dentist, do you automatically trust his dentist?

Public Key Infrastructure (PKI) architecture (for instance, the kind used by web sites that sell products) works the same way as personal certificates, in other words, Web of Trust. It's better than passwords at authentication. But web certificates and trust as they sell it is … a word that has been stricken from this page by the editor.

Why? Many reasons. Consider Verisign, probably the single largest seller of web security certificates. Verisign provides different levels of certificates that require higher levels of proof of your identity as you pay more for "better" certificates. How expensive a certificate would you have to buy for a representative of Versign actually to visit your business and confirm who you are? Think "cubic bucks" (or Euros or whatever). But anything less just opens the door to fraud. If Verisign is willing to sell me a basic certificate for cheap, and I fully intend to rip people off, what's to stop me? Once I get reported they'll revoke my certificate. By then I may be a millionaire. (Send your credit card numbers now!) So the mere fact that Verisign sold someone a certificate doesn't really assure anything. Just remember: their motive is profit, not necessarily your

---

benefit.

What's worse is that certificate and PKI vendors make really attractive targets. Consider the case of RSA Security, a major corporation that sells cool SecureID products, like little USB-stick-like devices that show a number in a little window, and you'll need that number in order to log in (when you need a user name, a password and a SecureID number, that's an example of **Multifactor Authentication**). You'd think RSA, which is after all a security company, would have a good handle on ... security. But no. They got hacked, a lot of their data was stolen, and a whole planet full of companies that used RSA security had to do some serious re-thinking.

Says one contributor, "Personally, I use GPG and even freeware PGP from pgpi.org. It works. I use TrueCrypt. I like encryption as it provides confidentiality and integrity to my messages. I use HTTPS because it encrypts my sessions. But I don't use HTTPS to validate that it's the right and proper website that I think I'm attaching to." Which is a whole 'nother problem....

Sending An Encrypted Email Using GPG

Most email clients support plugins that make the handling of keys and encryption easier. The best thing to do is to check beforehand if your recipient has a public key and get it from a key server, or from the recipient themself.

Then, compose your email as normal (once again we strongly recommend plain text email over HTML), add any attachments and tell your email client to encrypt and send the email. If you decided to sign the email, the email client will use your private key to sign the message first, then use the public key of your recipient to encrypt the email and any attachments. If you protect your key pair with a passphrase (you'd better!), your email client will ask for that passphrase.

Receiving An Encrypted Email Using GPG

Email encrypted with GPG contains either an attachment flagged as GPG, or has a block of text with a header that tells a GPG-capable email client it has just received an encrypted message. The email client will now access your private key (possibly via a password) and decrypt the message and any attachments. If the message was not encrypted with your public key this decryption will simply fail. If the message was signed by the sender, the GPG plugin will use the corresponding public key to verify that signature too.

GPG plugins will alert you to problems with signatures or attachments, but in general you will find that once installed, the use of GPG is quite easy.

GPG Implications

Be aware that the majority of email is not encrypted, and that probably includes your own. Some people think that using encryption is suspicious and draws attention all by itself. It's your right to have privacy when communicating, so don't worry too much about the opinions of others.

GPG is not easy to use in a webmail environment (aside from the obvious question whether you can trust a third party to encrypt properly and not mount a man in the middle attack on your secrecy) and also doesn't work well on mobile clients. Be wary of mobile apps that claim to solve this issue: some have been found to send your data elsewhere for processing!

There are online mail services that sell encrypted, "enhanced security" email accounts. But be careful to read the fine print on your user agreement. One provider's reads like this:

"I understand that this service is not suitable for illegal activity and that the providers of this service will cooperate fully with authorities pursuing evidence via valid legal channels."

Of course, "legal channels" include programs like Echelon, Carnivore, PRISM, the Patriot Act and XKeyscore. Look 'em up and ask yourself just how "enhanced" you think this paid "security" really is.

Some countries mandate that you must be able to decrypt any information when ordered to do so by court. For example, in the UK you can be served under the Regulation of Power Act 2000, and non-compliance is termed as contempt of court, automatically resulting in jail time. This has unpleasant implications: if you have been experimenting with encryption and have forgotten the keys or passwords, you will effectively face jail for being forgetful (yes, you will be guilty until you can prove your innocence). It is thus good practice to erase any encrypted material and email that you can no longer access. In a corporate setting you must manage and document key and passphrase changes and disposal of encrypted information very carefully.

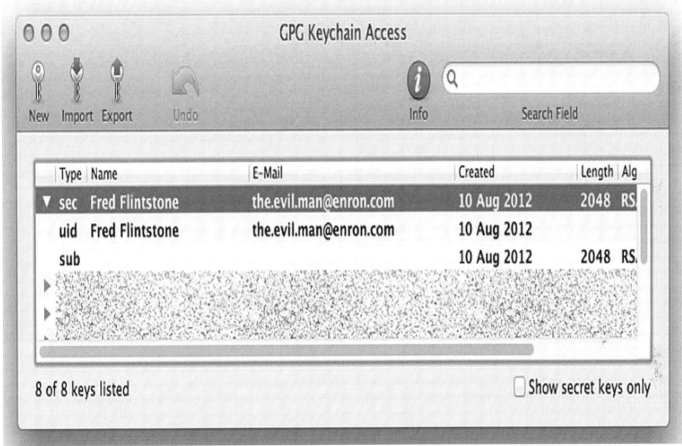

Figure 2.4: *The GPG Keychain*

Last but not least, it is interesting to note that the use of email addresses to identify a key is a **convention**, not a mandated standard. It is entirely possible to generate and use keys for email addresses that do not exist. Such keys are still accepted at public servers. This is known as "hiding in plain sight," and it means that there is no relation between the email addresses and the key used to encrypt/decrypt traffic. In the above image, for instance, both person and email address are fictitious.

The disadvantage of doing this is that it breaks an established way of working, and plugins such as **Enigmail** may need some convincing before they support this more creative approach. A further area for experimentation is expired keys: expiration doesn't stop the keys from working.

Exercises

2.8   Download the GPG support for your email client program and install it.

2.9   Find out how to generate your own key. Do so. Keep it local; don't accept any offers to upload your public key to a public key management server.

2.10 Add other email addresses to your key, then change the passphrase.

2.11 Now publish your public key to a key management server.

2.12 Compose an email to someone using GPG. How would you go about getting their key? Do it.

2.13 What can you do with messages when you only have your own key?

2.14 Create a new key for a fake email address. How easy is it to do on your machine?

Email Server-Side Vulnerabilities and Threats

Both small and large organizations use email servers to send and receive these electronic messages, unless they outsource the task or use a cloud service. Email serves multiple purposes to its users: some are good purposes and some are evil (hear madman laughing in the distance). Email servers are the first line of attack/defense on a network perimeter.

Emails have been used to send family vacation pictures, piano recital songs, birthday cards, have a bad day cards, homework assignments, excuses for not turning homework, company communications, marketing, newsletters and an assortment of other media. Besides the "Have a Bad Day" email, all the emails mentioned above have a friendly use. Email serves a valuable purpose for daily communications.

On the other hand, emails have been exploited to send out flame letters, porn, pirated MP3s, classified information, corporate research secrets, taunts, cyber bullying, malware, phishing, and spam. In 2012, email attachments moved to second place behind rogue web sites as the primary delivery tool for malware. A vital part of our communal society has become perverted for criminal use.

Feed Your Head: Keeping The (Server's) Lights On

The MED is an Educational Computer Lab at UTC (a University in Latin America). This lab is entirely run by students: selection, training, management, etc. It was created for two purposes: to manage the network used by the Computer Science department's teachers and fellow students (including the professor's desktops, the servers, switches, firewalls, the works) and to let students learn how to be sysadmins in a real world environment.

On Saturday morning, IO, one of the sysadmins, gets a call from Professor X from the CS department. He is in a rage because the email service isn't working and he has a paper due on Monday. He had already done the basic test like sending himself email from and to other email accounts. IO and PEEL (another sysadmins) get moving to the MED and start debugging the email server. After some analysis, they find that the problem is that **Exim** is crashing every time it tries to process the outgoing queue.

After the usual test of restarting the service and running the command by hand in the debug mode, they jump into analyzing the core with no real clue as to what's going on. They finally check how many emails were in the queue and find close to **100,000 emails!** With this in mind there is no doubt the server is being **DOS**ed. After a quick analysis of the mails in the queue, they see that the emails are all coming from a machine inside the MED. When they find the machine that is doing the damage the obvious is done: they pull out its network cable.

So the DOS is contained, and they jump into getting the service back. This was a no brainer, a simple Perl script. Later they are moving all the emails that match the attacker's IP address from the queue into another folder for later analysis. Once the folder is clean, they restart the service and all is well. The next step is to call up the student assigned to the offending workstation and ask what exactly he was doing. It turned out to be a watch-dog program that would send an email every two seconds reporting a lost connection, and to make things worse the team's email accounts were full so that emails started **bouncing** (failing to be delivered). After the storm the student fixed his code, the professor got his paper in on time and the sysadmins didn't get any glory as usual. By the way after this incident the mail service was migrated to **Postfix**, a more secure mail server. Which let them discover it's vulnerable to DOS too, unfortunately, but nothing's perfect, right?

Bandwidth Eating

Email servers should be configured to block the bad stuff and allow the good stuff to pass to you. This sounds easy enough and it will be easy for us to tell you about it. You'll have all the hard work of making it happen (again, mad scientist laughing in the distance). All email traffic coming and going through a network eats up vital bandwidth. You will never hear someone complain, "My connection is too fast." The sooner you can detect and inspect email traffic (outbound and especially inbound) on your email server, the less bandwidth is wasted. Besides preserving bandwidth, the ability to filter bad emails early on will save work on CPU server processing.

Some studies estimate that 80% of all inbound email is spam. Do you really want to wait until that junk gets into your email inbox before this stuff is detected and deleted? The sooner spam is intercepted by your email servers, the better. One technique used is when spam is detected, the server will eliminate it after a certain amount of time. This prevents deletion of email traffic that a user might be expecting. Your organization's marketing department might really want that one email with the subject line "How to improve your performance." Turn off automatic email confirmations and receipts to save bandwidth on the email server, too. Your users won't mind, trust us.

Since your email servers are access points exposed to attacks coming from the Internet, you should take extra precautions for anyone with admin rights. Those who have admin rights should never send or receive email while they are logged in with admin privileges. In fact, those with admin rights should only use those rights for internal network maintenance. Over the years, many networks have been compromised when an admin logged in and surfed the Internet or sent emails while working with escalated privileges.

Email Server Vulnerabilities

As the name might suggest, an email server is just like any other server. The server will have vulnerabilities that can be exploited. The Common Vulnerabilities and Enumeration database at http://cve.mitre.org listed a total of 1043 email server vulnerabilities in 2012. Many of these issues can be resolved through proper server configuration and user privileges. Other issues can only be solved by the software manufacture or by being vigilant when shopping for server software.

For a complete list of all known email server vulnerabilities go to http://cve.mitre.org/cgi-bin/cvekey.cgi?keywHacking_Emailord=email+server.

Email Server Threats

Large web email clients like Gmail, Yahoo, and Microsoft migrated to a new cryptographic email signature program called **DomainKeys Identified Mail (DKIM)**. DKIM wraps a cryptographic signature around an email that verifies the domain name that the message was sent through. DKIM helps filter out spoofed messages from legitimate ones. The specifications for DKIM can be found at http://www.dkim.org/.

The problem involves DKIM test messages. According to **US-CERT (United States Computer Emergency Readiness Team)**, an evil hacker can send a flag that it is testing DKIM in messages. Some recipients will "accept DKIM messages in testing mode when the messages should be treated as if they were not DKIM signed."

This isn't the first DKIM problem that has attracted CERN's attention. The signature key length used for encryption was vulnerable to cracking if the key size was too small. DKIM standards set the minimum key size to 1024, with any email using a smaller key being rejected by the program. But DKIM operations didn't reject smaller key sized emails. Instead, the emails were sent along their merry way, fully vulnerable to factor cracking. Once the key was cracked, a hacker could spoof emails or send out malware using that user's email key and address.

DKIM is designed to act as a "trust" verification tool for email. The system uses public-key cryptography, just like PGP does. With proper use, an email can be traced back to its original sender through a domain verification process. Basically, you are identifying yourself as the sender by your domain origin. This should drastically reduce spoofed emails, filter spam, and prove that you sent that message. Security folks call this non-repudiation.

In non-repudiation, the information provider data cannot be changed. The information is not refutable. If you said, "I want to wear a dress," that statement cannot be contested. You said it, that is a fact and you will not be able to retract that statement. This is important when dealing with contracts, legal matter and excuses to your father for not taking out the trash.

Feed Your Head: Hacking Email Servers With EXPN and VRFY

The first topic in every mail server security checklist is disabling the venerable **EXPN** and **VRFY** commands.

The EXPN command allows to expand an address associated to a list (i.e. an alias). It's usually a bad idea to allow it since it can be used for user enumeration and email addresses harvesting (which helps spammers). Also since some mail aliases can be a pipe to a program it would easily leak information about your operating system and software.

The VRFY command verifies if an email address is valid or not (without expanding it) on the SMTP session. This allows easy addresses enumeration since it's possible to use several VRFY commands on the same SMTP session and that it can be used without actually delivering a message.

Here's an example of how the two commands can be used against a too-friendly mail server:

```
# telnet mail.example.org 25
Trying 192.168.1.1...
Connected to mail.example.org.
Escape character is '^]'.
220 box.example.org ESMTP mail.example.org ; Mon, 9 Oct 2006 15:39:45 GMT
HELO testclient.example.org
250 mail.example.org Hello testclient.example.org [10.1.7.2], pleased to
meet you
expn root
250-2.1.5 <joe@mail.example.org>
250 2.1.5 <mike@mail.somewhereelse.com>
expn sales
250 2.1.5 <"|/usr/bin/mlmmj-receive -L /var/lists/example.org/sales/">
vrfy joe
250 2.1.5 <joe@mail.example.org>
vrfy notauser
550 5.1.1 notauser... User unknown
```

We can quickly gather that there are at least two administrators of the box ("joe" with a local mailbox and "mike" with a remote one) and that the sales alias points to a mailing list implemented with the mlmmj software. On the same SMTP session we also verified that joe@mail.example.org actually exists as well as confirming another nonexistent user.

Since the two commands are known to be related to malicious activity they tend to make noise in your server logs. Here's an example of sendmail's reaction:

```
Oct  9 15:40:26 mail sendmail[2885]: k99FosFv002885: testclient.example.org
[10.1.7.2]: VRFY root
```

```
Oct  9 15:40:28 mail sendmail[30666]: k99FdjD6030666: testclient.example.org
[10.1.7.2]: expn root
Oct  9 15:40:28 mail sendmail[30666]: k99FdjD6030666: testclient.example.org
[10.1.7.2]: expn sales
..
Oct  9 15:40:28 mail sendmail[30666]: k99FdjD6030666: testclient.example.org
[10.1.7.2]: expn admin
Oct  9 15:40:28 mail sendmail[30666]: k99FdjD6030666: testclient.example.org
[10.1.7.2]: possible SMTP attack: command=EXPN, count=6
```

Exercise

2.15   There is another command you can exploit: RCPT TO. What can you find out about this command? How could you use it to find email addresses?

Email for Fun and Profit

Thanks to the profitable market for corporate espionage, email is a simple method to find client contact lists, customer information, meeting notes, new product developments, answers to the next math test and all kinds of valuable data. We are not even going to get into government espionage, simply because we all know this has been taking place since the dawn of man. There are several primitive cave paintings depicting one caveman spying on another caveman's woolly mammoth with envy. One can only imagine the spy caveman returning to his tribe to describe the newest version of Mammoth 2.0.

A simple but often missed email security method is scanning of all email attachments. Scanning needs to be performed on all data packets, compressed files, unknown file types, split files, files that can do the splits, files that spit, meta data, files with URLs, and pretty much everything that can be done to a file. This scanning should be focused on inbound traffic but don't forget to be suspicious when large attachments are leaving your network. Sensitive company information needs to be encrypted, especially if sent by email, to anyone inside or outside the network. Oh, by the way, sensitive information really should never leave the network. If a user is sending information outside the network, you might want to keep an eye on their activities.

Large organizations like the Veterans Affairs Hospitals in the US use **data loss prevention (DLP)** software to do all this stuff. Never attempt to playfully email your ex's medical records from the VA Hospital, for instance, since the people who come play with you will make you wish you had just cut your throat and gone *straight* to ... well, you know where.

The Key to Success

Keyword filtering is a type of application layer filtering (layer 7) that lets you block all messages containing particular keywords or phrases (text strings) that commonly appear in spam (for instance, "Viagra" or "hot sexy babes"). Other forms of email filtering include:

- **Address blocking**: a filtering method that blocks mail from particular IP addresses, email addresses or domains of known spammers.

- **Bayesian filtering**: "intelligent" software that can analyze spam messages and learn to recognize other messages as spam using **heuristics** (patterns of behavior).

- **Blacklisting**: lists of known spammers' addresses can be shared, so each user doesn't have to develop a list from scratch. These lists are available from several providers, and are highly valuable for address blocking.

- **Whitelisting**: a filtering method that, instead of specifying which senders should be blocked, specifies which senders should be allowed. Again, these lists are used as part of address blocking.

- **Greylisting**: this temporarily blocks email from unknown sources. Legitimate email will be re-transmitted, but spam usually won't.

- **Challenge/Response filtering**: replies to email from senders not on a "trusted senders" list with a challenge, usually involving solving a task that is easy for humans but difficult for automated bots or scripts.

There are many open-source and for-pay applications that can do these kinds of filtering, some better and some worse. If you've ever had to deal with these PITAs (we'll let you figure out on your own what a PITA is) you'll see them as the challenges to clever script writers that they are.

Email Client-Side Vulnerabilities and Threats

Incoming email may contain malware, usually in the form or an attachment or a web link. When you see these clues think "Scam!"

- An unexpected origin: who sent you this mail, and would they have sent it? A favorite trick of spammers is to use other people's valid email address as the origin so spam passes filters and users are more likely to open the email.

- A "too good to be true" event such as a lottery win, inheritance or bank "mistakes" in your favor. Look up the "Nigerian scam." Do any of the sample messages you'll find look familiar? Practically everyone has gotten one.

- A domain mismatch between "from" and "reply-to" addresses (compare them).

- Weird, strangely incorrect or over-complex use of language.

- Unexplained or illogical urgency. (Why would this email be so urgent?)

- Embedded web links which go to different domains than the human readable text suggests (e.g. a link that appears to go to *www.bank.com* in reality goes to *www.l33thacker.org* with a fake banking site). Most mail clients now show the real website address when a mouse cursor is hovered over the relevant text.

- Attachments with active content, such as .exe or .html. These are especially risky on platforms that auto-execute content.

Exercise

2.16 Go to http://www.419eater.com/. What is scam baiting? Can you find instructions? Can you find *precautions*? This is dangerous stuff. Knowing about it doesn't mean you should do it. But you shouldn't be defenseless either.

Turn On The Lights

Email content is a wonderful way to get users to click on malicious links. One common tool is the **Blackhole Exploit Kit**. Sounds scary, doesn't it! Can you say "Blackhole Exploit Kit" five times really quick without making any mistakes? Blackhole is a web application exploitation program that takes advantage of known vulnerabilities in Java and Adobe applications. It's used to send a phishing email to users, trying to get the user to click on a compromised web link.

Phishing is an attempt to gather important information from a victim by using **social engineering**, persuasive emails sent out to thousands of users. Typical phishing emails appear to come from a well-known and trusted organization. The attackers will use the exact same logo, similar reply email address, and as much professional wording as they can to fool as many people as they can. The email will ask the reader to "verify" or "update" credit card data, personal bank account information and other stuff that you would only give to a trusted source.

When the victim clicks on the official-looking link, the link sends them to a compromised page where the malware payload is installed on their machine. The user is unaware they're being **pwned**, and not all anti-virus programs detect the installation. Once the payload is on the user's computer, the phishing spam senders now control that computer as well as any content they want to collect from it.

Blackhole spam pretends to come from legitimate companies like Amazon, Visa, Twitter, UPS and many organizations that wouldn't raise a user's suspicion. This program is rented by paying for server time on the Blackhole server. Recent fees ranged from $50 for a day to $150 a month.

Malware, Trojans, And Rootkits, Oh My

The media loves to play up email cracking, because fear sells. (Remember that when anyone who's selling you something tries to scare you.) But the truth is, malware has been around a long, long time.

Dr. Fred Cohen wrote his PhD dissertation on the idea of a computer virus in 1984, published it in 1985, and it was yanked from public viewing a few weeks later. 1985 was a long time ago and the media still acts like malware is a massive new threat to the entire world.

We are not going to tell you every transmittable threat; you can look them up yourself in Lesson 6, Malware. We are going to show you how email security works from both the inside and the outside.

This Email Looks Legitimate, Let's Open It Up

STOP!!!!! Don't open that email just yet. In fact, don't even preview the email. There are several ways email has been and is still used as an attack tool. Social engineering is the preeminent technique to get people to open email, open attachments or click on malicious web links inside an email or message. Social engineering preys on several human emotions we all have including curiosity, wanting to be helpful, trust in our friends, greed and many types of financial or medical concerns. See Lesson 20 for much more about social engineering.

Our curiosity with new or unknown information can be used to persuade us to do stupid things. When you're sent an email that has "Subject: Re: Re: Thanks!" if you're a typical user, you'll want to know why you're being thanked. In this case, you are being thanked ahead of time for opening up an email with a malicious payload.

These types of emails ask you to call a phone number, click on a URL in the message or do anything that can give away your goodies.

Exercises

Consider an email with this at the top:

```
from:        Mr Norman Chan <naveen.kumar@iitg.ac.in>

reply-to:    2259575299@qq.com

to:          (your email address)

date:        Mon, Nov 19, 2012 at 7:40 AM

mailed-
by:          iitg.ac.in
```

2.17   Would you respond to an email that has this in its subject line: "Hello,I'm Norman Chan,i have a bussiness worth 47.1M USD for you to handle with me?" The sender is "naveen.kumar@iitg.ac.in."

2.18   Investigate this email address to see if Norman Chan owns a business worth 47.1M. Also check the reply-to address, "2259575299@qq.com." DO NOT GO TO QQ.COM.

2.19   Max out your browser's security settings before attempting this. Do a little research into qq.com but do not go to this URL. DO NOT OPEN THIS URL. Based on your research of qq.com, would this site raise any alarms for you? Explain why.

Game On: Springing the Trap

Behind the closed door of the Chief's office Jace inspected his computer for physical tampering. She noticed some scuff marks around the bottom of the case from his shoes. Maybe he was kicking the machine. Either way, unless you were down on your hands and knees, you would never see the marks. She looked at the empty USB ports, made sure the CD/DVD drive didn't work since she disabled those devices on every police networked computer. Not only did they not work but they couldn't be used as a bootable device at the BIOS level (and the BIOS was password protected).

Jace checked to make sure the logon password was restricted to five attempts and the password wasn't easy to guess. That was a strict rule that she had a long fight with the chief about. In the end, she won that battle for harder passwords. No easy to guess passwords.

The service tag she'd put on the machine was intact so there wasn't any evidence of the case being opened. Sliding back in front of the keyboard, Jace checked port 25 (SMTP) and looked to see if any services were running that were unusual. All the ports reported that they were open which was used to throw off any external port scan. The ports were not open, they just reported that they were open. Every computer on the police network were designed to the same exact specifications so they all looked the same, inside and out.

Now that the basic tests were complete, Jace was ready to open up her red eyeglass case and turn on her cellphone WiFi scanner. The scanner didn't show any local signals in the 2.4 GHz or 5 GHz across multiple channels, except for the microwave oven in the police lounge and a baby monitor nearby. Jace did notice an odd burst pattern around 3.6 GHz but her phone WiFi wasn't capable of analyzing it.

"So hey, don't do anything different. Just keep working while I go check out the rest of the building. Oh, can you keep an eye on my cookies too," she asked slyly. The Chief was on a diet and the bag of treats was sitting on his desk.

He said, "You let me know as soon as you find anything. Let me do the dirty work because I don't want anyone coming after you in retaliation. Got it?" Jace just winked back and walked down the hallway towards the server room.

The large metal door was easy to unlock using the combination of her shoe size, waist measurement, and the last two digits of her student ID card. The hard part was getting the massive door to open, since it was a tight fit against the doorframe. She figured that when the door was slammed shut it must have scared the heck of anyone being interrogated there, since it used to be the "interview room." Jace envisioned some poor slob beaten with rubber bananas while being asked where he was the night of some murder.

First she grabbed the main intranet server logs and events and ran through them, looking for anomalies and errors. Netscan showed a few minor issues with packet resends, email bounces, and one recurring problem with the police chief's IP address being reset. She was going to have to look for answers at each workstation.

"It's time to get dirty," she mumbled, leaving her pack behind and locking the server room behind her. The red eyeglass case fit comfortably in her back pocket, even if it made her butt bigger.

Every computer she inspected was exactly where it was supposed to be, with the service tag intact and the USB ports and CD drives disabled. Cobwebs, sticky coffee stains, nasty old french fries and used staples collected on her hands, knees and in between the strands of her hair.

Jace backed out from behind one of the last computers and was met by the glowing face of the police chief. "Anything yet?"

"You scared the crap out of me," she replied. "I haven't found much. I'm gonna have to get creative."

The Chief asked, "What do ya mean creative?" In all of his years of working with criminals, he didn't trust anyone. It was part of his job to not trust anyone. Professional distrust had kept him and many of his police officers alive.

As Jace picked herself up from the dirty floor, dust bunnies clinging to her, the Chief caught a look into her eyes. For more than a moment, he was no longer a cop inspecting a person. He was a father, he was wounded by the pain he saw in her timber brown eyes. He's been there the night Jace's mother died, and he'd kept the case open as a favor to his old high school sweetheart, Oace. Jace might well have been his daughter, if things had worked out differently. He had to trust someone. It might as well be Jace.

Jace didn't like the way the Chief was tearing up as he looked at her. Maybe it was all the dust on her making his eyes swell up. The hacker broke off their stare as she ruffled the cobwebs out of her hair. She continued, "Well, I found a few minor issues in the server logs, but I didn't find anything odd with any of the work stations, so I think it's time we raise the stakes."

The Chief regained his posture, standing a good two feet taller than the teen. "If anyone is going to get hurt or maimed, I don't want to know anything about it. Just do what you have to do," he said as he handed her his office keys. "I'm heading home for the evening. I know you're going to work through the evening so I'm not going to bother to ask if you want a ride home. When you're done in my office, just leave the keys with the desk sergeant. He'll get you a ride home."

The Chief patted Jace on the shoulder and said something that he hadn't said in three decades. "I trust you." He walked toward the front hallway and left.

Now it was her turn to tear up. "It must be the dust," she told herself. It wasn't.

The hacker returned to the server room and grabbed a pencil and paper. She drew a flowchart of all the possible ways that someone could steal emails and all the things she had already checked. Everything matched. This was becoming an interesting puzzle.

Her cell phone rang. It was Mokoa. "Everything okay?" He said the school administration was furious at her getting the Chief of Police to give her a ride in the SWAT van and the principal to bring her cookies. Jace got a good laugh until she realized something: Cookies.

"Mokoa, I gotta go, you just gave me a great idea. Thanks, I'll try and save you some cookies."

Jace barely ended the call as she was racing to the Chief's office. The Chief had nine keys on his ring and all of them looked identical. The last key she tried was the one that opened the office door. "That's my luck," she thought to herself, "It's always the last key."

The Chief's computer was still on, password protected, but still on. Jace knew the password since she was the one who assigned it. Looking at her diagram one last time, she calculated all the different possibilities before she ran her creative script. Chewing on her lower lip, she thought, *This is either gonna flush out the email sniffer or the chief's gonna kill me.*

She turned off the lights, locked the office doors and left the police station for the evening, yawning.

Third period Language Betterment class bored the entire collection of twenty-eight high school students. Jace sat midway between the back of the class and the front, slightly off to one side nearest the exit. She was running last night's events through her head, wondering how her script was performing. An SMS message came in on her cellphone as she was replaying her actions. The message was from the police chief and read, "Need Ur help now. Go to office!" Oops, not good. But it did get her out of Language Betterment.

Jace was waiting in the school administrative office watching the Vice Principal spying on her from his desk. The school secretary was more obvious, asking the teen a dozen questions about how many crimes she committed last week or how old was she going to be when she was finally released from prison. Jace ignored her as she watched the front entrance for a police car to arrive, like a chariot whisking the princess away to an awesome castle.

No such luck. The police chief pulled up in front of the school and waved Jace over to the car. The secretary and the vice principal were waiting for the officer to use handcuffs or something on Jace.

Jace entered the vehicle before the school doors could close. The Chief shrieked, "What the heck did you do? Was this some sort of joke or did you intend to plant a mail bomb on our network?"

"Wait, hold on here chief. I can explain," she said as she pulled out her cellphone.

"It better be an amazing explanation because our entire network is crashed."

The officer was pushing his foot on the accelerator to head back to the station when Jace told him to stop. "I can tell you what is going on but take it easy," she pleaded.

"I'm all ears," the Chief said sarcastically as he turned left into the school's back parking lot and stopped.

"Chief, I set up an email bomb using your account on the email server. I knew this would slow down the network but it wouldn't shut it down completely. All these emails are addressed to you and they'll sit in the email server queue since your account's already full. Whoever's spying on your account won't be able to handle all those emails without a huge hard drive." Jace pitched her voice in the key of calm.

"What I need you to do is to keep an eye out for anybody who acts suspicious or freaks out. I overloaded your account, which will also overload the person who's stealing your emails." Jace sounded halfway convincing but the Chief still looked nervous.

He asked, "Will I lose all my emails?"

"No, no. Not that I know of anyways."

"What do ya mean not that you know of. I can't lose my emails," he complained.

"You won't. Your emails will be safe because I can filter out all the email bomb stuff after you catch the email snatcher. Don't worry, they're on the email server, waiting in the queue. You'll be fine. The suspect won't be because they couldn't have as much storage space as you have on your computer. Trust me. Look for anyone in your building who's acting odd today," Jace said to the police chief, tentatively placing a calming hand on his shoulder.

He seemed reassured and repeated exactly what Jace had told him to look for before he drove off. Jace was left to return to Language Betterment class.

Later, Mokoa sat next to his hacker friend in the cafeteria, disappointed by the bag of cookie crumbs she gave him. "You couldn't save me one single cookie?" he asked like he hadn't had one in months.

"Sorry dude, I need all that fuel to keep this engine running on all cylinders," she replied, pointing to her head. "Next time, I promise I'll save you some."

Her phone rang, echoing off the smooth floor and bland walls. She fumbled to answer the phone. Phones weren't allowed at school. Jace dropped down below the lunch table. "Hello?"

A familiar voice spoke, "Jace, we got 'em. I found the guy who was stealing my emails. He was using some gizmo plugged into one of those network wall jacks. Whatever it is seemed to store all my emails. I guess the officer freaked out when you overloaded my email account."

The cafeteria fell silent when Jace yelled out, "Way to go, Chief!"

When Jace had free time, she met with the Police Chief in his office. He closed his door and showed her the device. The email thief had plugged in an Ethernet splitter at the jack. The splitter was connected to a small netbook that was hidden behind a file cabinet. Jace had only checked each computer; she didn't think to check every jack. She added that to her mental checklist.

The Chief explained that the email thief scrambled to detach his homemade hack when everyone complained about the network slow-down. "He knew you were here and he worried that his gadget was causing the slowdown. One of our other officers noticed the thief messing around behind a file cabinet and saw the netbook. The email hacker was good friends with a suspect. That same officer was the one who didn't turn in the murder weapon and wanted to make sure nobody else turned in that weapon. That's why I got the phone call about the inventory. He was checking my emails to see if there was missing evidence, crafty guy."

The Police Chief handed Jace another large bag of homemade cookies. "Could you kindly remove the email bomb and get the network back up to speed?"

Game Over

Exciting Tricks With Email Systems (Hacking the Postman)

Email seems to always play some part when it comes to a security breach or a huge network attack. Every virus, every bit of malware, every phishing event seems to involve email as either a major transport mechanism or a way to enter a system to begin an attack. Email may not be as popular as other communication forms like SMS or IM, but it's what's used the most in the corporate and government world. Now we're going to look closely at the very idea of email and how it can be used as a weapon or a shield.

When mapping a network, we need to know several entry points. If we rely on just one entry point, what we do we do when that vulnerability gets patched or fixed? Multiple entry points to a network allow us more freedom to move around that network and give us more avenues of approach. Avenues of approach are a good thing, trust us.

Knowing the user name scheme used by an organization for email or network access gives us a major advantage. Once we know a user name, we can then focus on obtaining that user's password. Most, but not all, organizations use "firstname.last name@companyname.com. Some use variations of first initial and lastname@ companyname.com. Others use the last name followed by the first initial @companyname.com. Pretty lame, right? How much more lame is it when the email address is also the user's login name? This mistake is far too common.

Organizations have a directory within their network that allows users to know who's who and where they work or what they do. That internal directory is a gold mine of information for an attacker. You can look up people in Facebook or other social media to learn more about each user. You can find out when they're going on vacation, what they do, what their hobbies are and other clues to the types of passwords they would use. This information is also valuable if you want to pursue social engineering against that person (for fun and profit).

SEAK And Ye Shall Find

Let's look at gathering email addresses and using email as a hacking tool. Email hacking is closely linked with social engineering, just in case we haven't pointed that out enough already. The **Social Engineering Automation Kit (SEAK)** at http://www.seak.com.ar/ is designed to use search engines to locate email addresses in a network or on a web site. SEAK is basically a set of Perl scripts that allow search engines to look deep into web pages and networks then report back all the email addresses it finds. SEAK can also be used to locate people in the same way.

SEAK has a brother program at https://github.com/FreedomCoder/ESearchy-ng, called **Esearchy**. We didn't name it so don't blame us for the strange name. Esearchy does the same things as SEAK but does it in a Windows environment and searches documents too. Esearchy looks for passwords hidden in metadata, along with any other useful information like email addresses that are available to the public.

Another tool, **Maltego**, is an open-source intelligence and forensics analyzer. It provides tools for discovering data from open sources, and showing that information as a graph, which is handy for link analysis and data mining. The whole point is analyzing real-world relationships between people, groups, websites, domains, networks and online services like your favorite social networks.

An easy tool that you may have heard of is Google search. If you want to see all the employee profile information for a company you can use this command:

```
site:www.google.com intitle:"Google Profile" "Companies I've worked for" "at
company_name"
```

If you want to search all email addresses in a domain or URL, you can use Esearchy. You'd type the following all on one line, substituting a real domain for "company."

```
esearchy -q"@company" -y
AwgiZ8rV34Ejo9hDAsmE925sNwU0iwXoFxBSEky8wu1viJqXjwyPP7No9DYdCaUW28y0.i8pyTh4
```

```
-b 220E2E31383CA320FF7E022ABBB8B9959F3C0CFE --enable-bing --enable-google
--enable-yahoo --enable-pgp -m 500
```

Gpscan is a Ruby application that can automate this search and produce even more results. When paired with the command above, Gpscan becomes a powerful script tool for reconnaissance and social engineering. You can find Gpscan at http://www.digininja.org/projects/gpscan.php.

While you're using any of these, take the time to learn how these tools work. Pay particular attention to the syntax available for each tool and what each one does. You can learn quite a lot about how search engines can be used to hunt for and return email addresses, and possibly a few passwords. Also know which engines are used for the job. Some of the best search engines on the Internet are difficult to find.

Exercises

2.20 Now it's time for you to research a security tool on your own. Find **FOCA** (the metadata tool). What does it do? Would you want it as an arrow In your quiver?

Spoofing Versus Malware

In 2007, the CEO of a Fortune 500 company received an email that appeared to be from one of his senior staff. The email's **From:** line showed that the email was sent by a close associate. The **Subject:** line said something like, "How to reduce energy costs." When the CEO opened the email he saw an attachment and a link that also appeared to be legitimate. The CEO opened the attachment and didn't see anything on his screen so he closed the email.

Several months later, the FBI met with that same CEO to tell him that several terabytes of data had been stolen from his company due to a malware infection from the CEO's machine. The FBI confirmed which email had the malware attachment and that "How to reduce energy costs" was the culprit. The message had been spoofed.

This situation happens every day. Your uncle will call you and ask, "Why are you sending me so many email ads?" At school, your buddy keeps getting spam from you for useless products. Why are you sending out all these spam messages?!

You're not.

Your email address has either been spoofed or your computer email program has been hacked. To find out whether an email address was spoofed, you will need to look at the email header of the sent email. We talked about this already. Now let's put your knowledge to work.

Ask anyone who received a spam email from you to FWD it to you, whole, not just by quoting the message. The header will tell you if your email address was spoofed or not. Look at the **Reply** and **Sent** portion of the email. As we already saw in previous exercises, the header will show that the email was either sent by you - or by someone else.

Stupid Email Tricks

When it comes to privacy, web based email is anything but private. The web service can be asked to provide all of your emails, contacts, calendars and such, if presented with legal documents showing a cause to release that data. One old but still useful trick is to create a web email account using some name other than your own. Whoever you are sending secret emails to has the same access to the account as you. You create your email and save it as a draft. You never send the email, just create a draft of the contents. The email stays in your account but is not traceable since it was never sent. Your partner logs into the same account and read the draft email. Once read, the draft can be deleted or altered to create a new draft email for you to read. It's like Ping-Pong without a ball. The same can be done with a shared Google Doc, by the way.

> **NOTE:** You don't get to be the director of the United States Central Intelligence Agency without knowing this little trick.

The email meta data is actually outlined in RFC 2822. Someone thought that it was a good idea to include meta data in email! What medication were they on when they thought this one up? The email meta data can include the following information:

- To
- From
- CC
- BCC
- Date

- Subject
- Sender
- Received
- Message-ID
- References
- Resent
- Return-Path
- Time/Date
- Encrypted
- In-Reply-To

Okay, don't worry too much about RFC 2822 on email meta data. The reason is, the RFC only covers electronic text traffic. Your SMS texts, all your Instant messages, and those photos you shared contain this wonderful invasion of your privacy, as well. However, this hidden data is covered under a different RFC. Listen to the sound of the evil scientist laughing once again in the background. "Wha ha, ha, ha, snort, ha, ha, ha, snort, ha, ha ha - Igor get me a tissue."

Outsmarting The Email Bots (Email Obfuscation)

This is so simple that you will laugh at yourself for not thinking of this earlier.

When you need to send your email address to someone else or to some account or some other crazy reason; are you going to send it in plain text? If you do, you're opening yourself up to spambots. These spambots are vicious creatures that have mother issues and they slime their way through the Internet looking for email addresses.

It's like connecting a brand new computer to the Internet without enabling any security features: An email address sent in plain text is just asking for trouble. You might as well connect a J-2 crossover to the Viper 115 ROJ input module inside a .002 latent relay link with a Blast Ion K-0a801 inside a quad reverberator! How messed up is that! Bad idea, very bad idea.

To outsmart these, you might want to try altering your email address when you send it. As with anything else, there is a trade-off between ease of use and security. There are several techniques, just use your imagination.

somebodyatsome.whereelse

Somebody@somedotwhereelse

somebody2some.whereelse

These have been used successfully to pass on an email address and bypass those weak bots. We'll see how long that lasts.

Exercises

2.21 Look at Etherios EasyDescribe from http://appexchange.salesforce.com. This is a free metadata viewer/extractor. Grab some of those emails you have stashed away and run them through Etherios. What metadata is in those emails that is not in the header?

2.22 If some data is not in the header, where could that metadata be hidden in the email?

2.23 Does RFC 2822 require metadata to be embedded in electronic text or is it just a standardized method for Internet email traffic?

2.24 Using whatever means you think is best, try and locate the correct business email address of the three company CEOs listed below. Hint, first find out who they are.

1. Coca Cola

2. Kia

3. British Aerospace Engineering (BAE)

Feed Your Head: The Ultimate Disclaimer

Contributor Peter Houppermans, author of *The Evil Guide to Privacy*, wrote us to say:

If you ever feel the need to highlight the folly of email disclaimers, please find here one Peter Houppermans cobbled together from very old USENET posts together with some of his own. A critical part of being a successful hacker is having a functional sense of humor: not only does it make you unpredictable, it also provides armor against those times when IT gets the better of you. Laugh, dust yourself off and rejoin the fight. Computers cannot win; we'll unplug them:

> The opinions expressed herein are those of the author, do not necessarily represent those of his employer or someone else, are probably silly, and have nothing to do with the recent consumption of liquor to the value of the GDP of a small country.

> The information in this email and any attachments is purely nonsensical and unlikely to be politically correct. It is intended solely for the attention of world + dog and its mother. I sincerely believe it's totally pointless to tell you what to do with this email if I managed to send it to the wrong place. This email does not contain nudity (yet), and no cuddly animals or whales were hurt during its production as there weren't any available. In true consulting style this email has been composed entirely from recycled keystrokes and cut-n-paste from many, many other leaving emails and other versions to other audiences (minus the embarrassing parts - I take PayPal, hint). May harm the digestive system if swallowed (especially when printed on cardboard), batteries not included. Author may sue, contents may settle. For more culture, add yoghurt. Unsuitable for people under 18 or those lacking an operable sense of humour. Do not hold upside down, open other end. If you received this email in error, well done.

> Any attachments should not be trusted or relied upon, but may prove highly entertaining.

> This disclaimer is meant for educational purposes only. Send no money now. Ask your doctor or pharmacist. To prevent electric shock, do not open back panel. No user serviceable parts inside. You may or may not have additional rights which may vary from country to country. Not recommended for children under twelve years of age. Batteries not included. Limit 1 per customer. Does not come with any other figures. Any resemblance to real persons, living or dead, is purely coincidental. Keep away from open flame or spark. Void where prohibited. Some assembly required. All rights reserved.

List each check separately by bank number. Contents may settle during shipment. Use only as directed. Parental discretion advised. No other warranty expressed or implied. Unauthorized copying of this signature strictly prohibited. Do not read while operating a motor vehicle or heavy equipment. Postage will be paid by addressee. In case of eye contact, flush with water. Subject to approval. This is not an offer to sell securities. Apply only to affected area. May be too intense for some viewers. Do not fold, spindle, or mutilate. Use other side for additional listings. For recreational use only. Shipping and handling extra. No animals were harmed in the production of this signature. Do not disturb. All models over 18 years of age. If condition persists, consult your physician. Freshest if consumed before date on carton. Prices subject to change without notice. Times approximate. No postage necessary if mailed in Singapore. If swallowed, do not induce vomiting. Breaking seal constitutes acceptance of agreement. For off-road use only. As seen on TV. We reserve the right to limit quantities. One size fits all. Do not leave funds without collecting a receipt. Many suitcases look alike. Contains a substantial amount of non-active ingredients. Colours may, in time, fade. We have sent the forms which seem to be right for you. Slippery when wet. This product is only warranted to the original retail purchaser or gift recipient. For office use only. Net weight before cooking. Not affiliated with the Red Cross. Surfaces should be clean of paint, grease, dirt, etc. Drop in any mailbox. Edited for television. Keep cool; process promptly. $2.98/min AE/V/MC. Post office will not deliver without postage. Simulated picture. List was current at time of printing. Penalty for private use. Return to sender, no forwarding order on file, unable to forward. Do not expose to direct sunlight. Not responsible for direct, indirect, incidental, or consequential damages resulting from any defect, error, or failure to perform. No Canadian coins. Do not puncture or incinerate empty container. See label for sequence. Prices subject to change without notice. Do not write below this line. Time lock safe, clerk cannot open. At participating locations only. Serial numbers must be visible. Align parts carefully, then bond. Falling rock zone. Keep out of reach of children. Lost ticket pays maximum rate. Your cancelled check is your receipt. Check paper path. Place stamp here. Avoid contact with skin. Sanitized for your protection. Be sure each item is properly endorsed. Penalty for early withdrawal. Sign here without admitting guilt. No solicitors. Slightly higher west of the Mississippi. Storage temperature: -30 C (-22 F) to 40 C (104 F). Employees and their families are not eligible. Beware of dog. Contestants have been briefed on some questions before the show. No purchase necessary. Limited time offer, call now to ensure prompt delivery. You must be present to win. No passes accepted for this engagement. Extinguish all pilot lights. Processed at location stamped in code at top of carton. Shading within a signature may occur. Use only in well-ventilated areas. Replace with same type. Accessories sold separately. Booths for two or more. Check here if tax deductible. Keep away from fire or flame. Some equipment shown is optional. Price does not include taxes. Hard hat area. Pre-recorded for this time zone. Reproduction strictly prohibited. Adults 18 and over only. Detach and keep for your reference. No alcohol, dogs, or horses. Demo package, not for resale. List at least two alternate dates. First pull up, then pull down. Call toll free before deciding. Driver does not carry cash. Some of the trademarks mentioned in this product appear for identification purposes only. Record additional transactions on back of previous stub. This supersedes all previous notices. Tag not to be removed under penalty of law.

If you've read all the way to here you're either exceptionally curious. Or a lawyer.

Conclusion to Hacking Email

Now that you are thoroughly educated (or confused) about email, you can quickly see that this simple communication tool is not very simple at all. The way email works through systems can become quite complex and requires you to meet certain criteria. Remember how we sent you as an email through the typical send, route and receive process. You did pretty well, too. You might want to consider a career as an email. Just a thought.

Email etiquette is important since writing and sending off an email written when you were angry or upset could cause you trouble later on. Stop sending everyone CC'd replies. If you are going to respond to a bunch of folks, use BCC to protect others' email address privacy.

Along the same lines of protecting privacy, we discussed using encryption tools like PGP or GPG to send and receive emails away from prying eyes. The cool part of that section was actually creating a key to use for real. It wasn't all that painful was it? If you answered "yes," sorry. We are certain that the local fast food restaurant is still hiring, since security just isn't your thing. We hope that you didn't answer "yes," because we need as many security experts as we can get.

After that section, we went into heavy security topics. Ok, maybe they weren't all that hard core but we thought you would enjoy some of it. You have to admit that email server and client-side vulnerabilities and threats were fun! Well, we had fun writing it. We got to look at spam, spam and more spam. We know that it eats up valuable bandwidth so you need to filter it as soon as possible in the routing chain. We also know that the state of

Hawaii consumes more real Spam annually than any other state or country. They like their Spam.

Dig is an important email tool for Linux and Unix users for tracking down specific information. If you see large chunks of data leaving your network as email attachments, you know to take a closer look to ensure company secrets aren't part of those emails. One interesting point we discussed was the use of Blackhole server to exploit vulnerabilities within networks. This tool was been widely used for sending malware in email, knowing that someone in the domain is likely to open that email or click on the infected link within that electronic document. This kind of threat can be stopped by filtering email traffic and educating users on this issue. User education is a key element in security.

At this point in a conclusion you would get some advice that may or may not interest you. Not here. Just know that email security is a challenge to cyber security. How you view that fact depends on which side of the fence you're on.

Hacking Web Security and Privacy

Introduction to Web Hacking

What you do on the World Wide Web (the Web) is your own business, isn't it? You might think so, but it's just not true. What you do on the web is about as private and anonymous as where you go when you leave the house. You'd think your comings and goings are your own business, and the people of ISECOM would agree with you. But in most countries government and private investigators are free to follow you around, collecting data on where you go, whom you meet, and what you say. The focus of this lesson is learning how to protect yourself on the web and to do that, you will have to know where the dangers are.

Web security is a whole lot more than making sure your browser doesn't collect tracking cookies. In this lesson we hope to show you how deep the web actually goes. When most people think of the Internet they think of the web. Since you have already read some of the other lessons, you know that this isn't true. The world wide web is just a small fraction of the digital communication structure we know as the Internet. With web security we have to look at web servers, the software running on both the client and the server-side, as well as all the services we depend on. Our phones are the most connected devices ever made, yet few people understand the difference between Java and Javascript.

The code of most web applications is no longer just Hyper Text Mark Up Language (HTML), either. Entire operating systems are being used to enhance your online experience to sell you things or just collect personal information about you. Those pictures you post to your friends on social media are being used by other entities. You are unknowingly part of the largest privacy invasion ever created. And you are the one providing all the information.

Our focus here is not to scare you but rather educate you about how far web security really goes. We will cover the foundation of web applications, their uses and misuses, vulnerabilities, security practices plus some tricks of the hacking trade. As always, Hacker Highschool is not here to teach you criminal techniques. We endeavor to show you how to be security conscience. You must think on your own and learn on a continuous basis about the world around you.

Your phone, computer, tablet, vehicle and even home appliances are connecting to the internet whether you know it or not. Wouldn't you like to know what they are saying about you along with the data that is being collected? We hope to show you ways to protect your privacy and personal data. Perhaps you will take up the challenge and begin teaching others as the Institute for Security and Open Methodologies (ISECOM) does. Education is a powerful weapon.

Fundamentals of Web Security

The focus of this lesson is learning how to protect your privacy on the web and how to keep your own web sites safe against intelligent attacks. To do that, you will have to know where the dangers are and how to bypass those dangers. Our topic here is going to expose you to the massive security challenges facing web site owners. You probably heard about attacks such as SQL injections, buffer overflows, cross site scripting and more. This lesson is going to demonstrate what these attacks really mean to you as well as methods to exploit/defend each web based vulnerability.

First off, you need to understand that the original idea behind the Internet was to link academic organizations with certain **U.S. Department of Defense (DoD)** organizations. This basically meant that the Internet (**ARPANET**) was built on the premise that security wasn't needed, since you already had to be either a research university or a government entity to connect to the network. The original Internet linked a bunch of big computers all over the U.S. to each other so security wasn't really an issue, the availability and durability of these connections were some of the real concerns.

This is where the **Transport Control Protocol (TCP)** was first introduced to deliver packets of data from one big (really big, like we are talking about a computer the size of your garage) computer to another big computer far away. Way back then, nobody thought the Internet would ever get as large as it has today. **Internet Protocol** V4 (IP as in TCP/IP v4) addressing used a 32 bit number sequence which limited addresses to a specific amount of addressable devices (4,294,967,296 addresses, to be exact). Remembering that back then there were only so many universities and defense organizations that would need an IP address. The idea was to have a connection of computers that would provide information to anyone connected to it. The logic back then was "why would anyone ever want to limit the freedom of information exchange?"

Along came private companies that connected to the Internet. Soon, others followed and more and more became all part of the Internet we see today. However, since security wasn't part of the original plans for the Internet, we have many security challenges that keep us security experts nicely employed. Keep reading and you will have the skills you need to earn a good paying job as well.

You may have heard the phrase "Keep It Simple, Stupid", or KISS for short when it comes to planning or performing a task. One fundamental law of engineering is that "complexity causes failures" so you want to try and keep your design planning as simple as possible. In security, we just shorten the whole phrase to "Complexity Breeds Insecurity".

The **World Wide Web** has evolved into an extremely complex system of interconnected computers, weird wires & cables, sloppy software, and a few really bad people who want to take things that do not belong to them. This whole mess we think of as the web sits poorly balanced on top of an ancient architecture built when security was not an issue nor was it designed into the original plans. Think of the web as a single car train with millions of other train cars stacked onto of each other's roof, each using different construction material, with the original train half leaning off the tracks.

Yes, security professionals have our work cut out for us. You can be sure that employment in the security field will continue to rise in the years to come. Why? Because the Internet is a bullet train moving at light speed and expanding even faster. Too many people depend on the Internet each and every day to allow engineers time to rebuild the Internet from scratch. We can't repair the train's engine while the whole thing is still moving, so we lubricate the wheels a bit or we dust off some gauges. The Internet train has to continue running until the neighbors build some other new Internet using spare parts from the one we have now. Until then, work on your resume.

How the Web Really Works

The web seems pretty simple: you get onto the Internet, open a browser, type in a website URL, and the page appears. But the devil's in the details, and some of them can hurt you. So how does the web really work?

A quick trip to the fine folks who make standards for the web, the **World Wide Web Consortium (W3C, at http://www.w3.org)**, will teach you all you want to know about how the web works. Don't miss the history of the web at **http://www.w3.org/History.html**. The problem seems to be that definitions and standards might teach you how to be safe. But, probably not. The people who want to hurt you don't follow standards or laws.

Reality Check

So what really happens when you go to a website? Assuming you are already connected to the Internet, here's how it works step by step:

1. You open your browser (Explorer, Firefox, Chrome, Opera, Safari, or any number of other browsers out there).

2. You type in the **Uniform Resource Locator (URL)** into the browser's address line (the website address, like ISECOM.org; the real nerds often call them URI for **Uniform Resource Indicators**).

3. The website's URL is saved in the browser's history on the hard disk. Yes, there's a record of everywhere you've been, right there on your hard drive.

4. Your computer asks your default **Domain Name Server (DNS)** to look up the IP address of the website. The DNS connects the name www.ISECOM.ORG to the IP address of 216.92.116.13. Use www.Whois.net to locate detailed information on a web page and try a Reverse IP lookup to find the actual numbered address instead of the site names.

5. Your computer connects to the website's server, at the IP address it was given by the DNS, to TCP port 80 for "**http://**" websites, or TCP port 443 if you go to an "**https://**" secure web site. If you use https:// there are more steps like getting server certificates that we won't cover in this example.

6. Your computer requests the page you ask for (like History.html), or if you specify a folder the web server sends a default page, usually index.html. It's the server that decides this default file, not your browser.

7. Your IP address, the web page you are visiting and details about your browser are likely to be stored on the web server and/or proxy servers in between (see below).

8. The requested web page is stored in the browsers **cache**. Yes, there's a copy of every page you've visited, right there on your hard drive, unless the web server explicitly asks your browser not to store it (cache is often disabled for protected web pages served through HTTPS, or at least it should be).

9. Most web pages contain other elements, like pictures, ads, style sheets (instructions to your browser on how the page should be displayed), **Javascript**

(little programs, to do checks or make the web page look fancy and smooth). All these elements are retrieved in a similar manner as typing a URL by yourself.

10. The browser nearly instantaneously shows you what it has stored in your browser's cache. There's a difference between "perceived speed" and "actual speed" during your web surfing. This is the difference between how fast something is downloaded (actual) and how fast your browser and computer can render the page and graphics to show them to you (perceived). Remember: Just because you didn't see web page elements doesn't mean it didn't end up in your browser's cache.

The World Wide Web (web) is a massive **client-server network**. Clients are typical users who run web browsers to display or capture Internet data. Servers are web servers, such as Internet Information Server (IIS) on Windows or Apache on Unix/Linux. So the browser asks for a page, and the web server returns content in the form of **Hyper Text Markup Language (HTML)** pages.

Security - Here to Save the Day

Where does security come in? Well, if you're running a public web server, it's sort of like a retail store window. The front window is a great place to advertise and display your goods, however you don't want that store window left open so passers-by can take things for free. Ideally, you'd make sure that if someone throws a brick, your window doesn't shatter, either! Unfortunately, web servers operate complex software, and you can't have complex software without getting some bugs as well. Less scrupulous members of society will exploit these vulnerabilities to access data they shouldn't have access to (like credit card information, your medical records, and those pictures of you with the black eye that your little sister gave you). More on these vulnerabilities later.

Your browser *will* have vulnerabilities as well, and to make things worse, the creators of your web browser has its own agenda. Some bad Web sites can inject malicious code into your browser, or employ malicious links that can infect your computer. And let's not forget social media sites that watch your every move as well as collect every picture you post and every word you type. Last year, one specific social media site sold every bit of data they collected on its users to seven different companies. That social media site didn't lose FACE with their users though, since this massive sale of personal data wasn't listed in many BOOKs at that time.

Exercises

4.1 Locate your browser's cache and temp files. Examine the directory and the files inside. What is in those directories? How could this data be used against you? Is there a way to prevent the browser from caching files, or to clear the temp and cache when you close the browser?

4.2 Where can you find your browser's history file? Look at that history. What does it tell you about yourself? Is there a way to prevent the browser from recording this history? How can you clear this history?

4.3 Most on-line businesses collect a lot of information about you, which may seem harmless yet it becomes a privacy concern over time. Install the Firefox add-on called Ghostery. What does it do? What does it tell you?

4.4 Locate your favorite web sites and try to learn as much as you can about them. Who owns those sites? Where are the web servers located (physical location)? How long have those IP addresses been registered and who is listed as the Registrant Name?

4.5 When does your favorite web site domain name expire and can you purchase that domain name when it expires?

Game On: Who Hacked The Website?

"It's not like you were going to be the only person with access to the police web site. I've known you for years now and I don't even trust you with my electronics," Mokoa reasoned with Jace. He subconsciously braced himself next to the junky old metal police desk just in case Jace decided to smack him again. That previous hit almost cost them their relationship. Luckily Jace had learned the value of their friendship then, and she wasn't about to screw that up again, ever.

Without looking up from the monitor Jace replied, "Agreed, but I didn't give anyone here any password information about their web site. I just set it up and figured that they wanted me to maintain it. Hell, I built their entire network here for free. Nobody ever asked me for admin rights or passwords except for individual user accounts. I am root."

As the two teens crowded into the former police interview room recently converted into a server area, the puzzled hacker behind the keyboard was more interested in recovering the web site post-attack. Mokoa was concerned about who had accessed the police web console and created a back-up in the public directory. Jace was working in the digital world while Mokoa was thinking in the real world. They were a good team.

A blast of fresh air hit the small room as Officer Hank pushed into the room with the teens. "Hey Jace, how's it coming along and who is this handsome guy next to you? Do I need to frisk him for weapons, like chocolate or flowers?" Hank asked in a fatherly manner.

Mokoa stood up in reaction to the unexpected police officer standing over him. Actually, Officer Hank was towering over Mokoa. Hank held out his meaty hands to either shake Jace's friend's hand or place it manly on his shoulder. Mokoa started to introduce himself, "Hi I'm Mo."

"Mokoa, yeah. I've seen you a few times. Jace tells me all about you. I think she likes you," Hank gave a light jab at Jace's shoulder to soften his joke about her liking Mokoa.

"Shut up you two, I'm trying to work here," Jace growled back. Both guys stepped back from the cranky girl and shared a laugh at her reaction.

Jace confronted Officer Hank while looking at the screen and not at him, "You wanna tell me who in this building has admin access to this network besides me? Or more to the point, who screwed up the web site? I worked my butt off trying to make this network and web content perfect for you cops and all I get is this mess."

The burly police officer interrupted Jace, "Hold on their Miss High and Mighty. First off, you forgot to give anyone here the passwords to update the site. Secondly, we needed to add more information to our network. And C, you haven't been around lately to help make those changes happen. So you need to just chill out and remember that I've got a wooden baton and you don't."

Jace, put in her place, Mokoa thought with a slim smile. *By a cop, too. I like this guy.*

The flustered teen flopped back into the creaky old desk chair. She explained what she knew about how the web attack happened, what she had to restore and how the issue needed to be corrected. Hank squatted down next to her listening with interest. Every now and then, Mokoa added additional details.

Officer Hank explained his situation, "The chief wants dynamic content as part of the public web site. He wants things like traffic web cams, weather reports, most-wanted criminals, community volunteer patrol details and all kinds of stuff. He wants our web to give the users real-time information about events as they happen."

Jace sat leaning against the dilapidated police interrogation desk to absorb all this. She asked, "Okay, we can do all that. Now I need to know how you guys want me to implement the dynamic content. We could use Ruby on Rails, PHP, jQuery and HTML5 with push or pull data. What's your flavor?"

Hank just started back at Jace, blank look on his face.

A long pause, too long for Mokoa, was broken when Jace tilted her slender head and continued the conversation in a slower voice, "There are plenty of security concerns with any dynamic content we use. First, we have the top three application level issues. They sound like a crappy movie script."

Mokoa looked away. Jace spun around to face the computer screen. "Our biggest three issues with dynamic content are SQL injection, cross-site scripting and leaving unnecessary services running inside web applications. SQL injection is passing SQL code into an application. Potential attack strings are built from fragments of SQL syntax. They get executed on the database server side if the Web application doesn't screen out potential code. For example, we can have problems if we don't protect ourselves against malicious input like a single-quote character, which could close the SQL string and give the attacker unintended system and application access."

Without taking a breath, Jace continued as she typed," The easiest way to see how this works is to type this string for the e-mail address and password in a web form input and put a space at the end, noobs always forget that space."

```
' OR '1' = '1
```

"The condition will be satisfied by the always-true condition '1' = '1', the SQL statement will show us everything in the current table and the login will succeed."

Jace tossed her hair out of her face and pressed forward: "In order to eliminate this vulnerability, we need to pass the name and password to the database in a way that special characters aren't interpreted as part of the SQL command. The easiest way to do this is to avoid constructing ad hoc SQL statements, and instead pass the e-mail address and password as parameters to a stored procedure. Basically we tell the SQL database what an email address should look like and only accept valid inputs."

Hank and Mokoa hated feeling stupid around Jace but that was something they were both getting used to. The police office tried, "Great to hear that you know so much about these web security problems. But, can you fix all this stuff and give the chief the type of web site he wants?"

She squared up her shoulders like a soldier given a proper order. Jace answered back, "Hank, I'm on it. Don't you worry. I'll take care of everything, dude."

Hank smirked and thought, *That's what I'm worried about, dude.*

Game continues...

Rattling the Locks

Assume you have put up your own web server to host your blog, personal website, photos and whatnot. How could all that information be exploited and used against you? Let's find out, shall we?

Standard HTML pages are transferred using **Hyper Text Transfer Protocol (HTTP)**. It's a simple text-based system for connecting to a server, making a request and getting an answer. This means that we also can connect easily to a server using command line tools like **telnet** and **netcat**, and get information about what software is running on a specific server. Look at what you get when you run this simple two-line command:

```
netcat isecom.org 80    [now press <Enter>]
HEAD / HTTP/1.0          [now press <Enter> twice]
HTTP/1.1 200 OK
 Date: Wed, 29 Feb 2012 23:25:54 GMT
 Server: Apache/2.2.22
 Last-Modified: Tue, 07 Feb 2012 18:41:18 GMT
 ETag: "3dad-4b8641fe22f80"
 Accept-Ranges: bytes
 Content-Length: 15789
 Identity: The Institute for Security and Open Methodologies
 P3P: Not supported at this time
 Connection: close
 Content-Type: text/html
```

Every web server and version will return different information at this request – an IIS server will return the following:

```
netcat www.microsoft.com 80
HEAD / HTTP/1.0
HTTP/1.1 200 OK
 Connection: close
Date: Fri, 07 Jan 2005 11:00:45 GMT
Server: Microsoft-IIS/6.0
P3P: CP="ALL IND DSP COR ADM CONo CUR CUSo IVAo IVDo PSA PSD TAI TELo OUR
SAMo CNT COM INT NAV ONL PHY PRE PUR UNI"
 X-Powered-By: ASP.NET
 X-AspNet-Version: 1.1.4322
 Cache-Control: public, max-age=9057
 Expires: Fri, 07 Jan 2005 13:31:43 GMT
 Last-Modified: Fri, 07 Jan 2005 10:45:03 GMT
 Content-Type: text/html
 Content-Length: 12934
```

Getting More Details

You can take this further and obtain more information by using the "OPTIONS" modifier in the HTTP request:

```
netcat isecom.org 80    [now press <Enter>]
OPTIONS / HTTP/1.0       [now press <Enter> twice]
```

```
HTTP/1.1 200 OK
 Date: Fri, 07 Jan 2005 10:32:38 GMT
 Server: Apache/1.3.27 Ben-SSL/1.48 (Unix) PHP/4.2.3
 Content-Length: 0
 Allow: GET, HEAD, POST, PUT, DELETE, CONNECT, OPTIONS, PATCH, PROPFIND,
PROPPATCH, MKCOL, COPY, MOVE, LOCK, UNLOCK, TRACE
 Connection: close
```

This gives you all of the HTTP commands (or "methods") to which the server will respond in a specific directory (in this case "/", the root directory of the web server or "document root").

Notice that HTTP is completely "in the clear"; everyone can see what you're browsing for. Consider how this might be changed; look up and learn about "secure searching".

Doing all of this by hand is rather tedious, and matching it manually against a database of known signatures and vulnerabilities is more than anyone would want to do. Fortunately for us, some very enterprising people have come up with automated solutions like **nikto**.

Nikto is a **Perl** script that carries out various tests automatically. It runs a scan and provides a detailed report:

```
        ./nikto.pl -host www.hackerHigh School.org
- Nikto v2.1.5
---------------------------------------------------------------------
+ Target IP:            216.92.116.13
+ Target Hostname:      www.hackerHigh School.org
+ Target Port:          80
+ Start Time:           2012-03-20 13:33:49 (GMT-6)
---------------------------------------------------------------------
+ Server: Apache/2.2.22
+ ETag header found on server, fields: 0x2f42 0x4b8485316c580
+ Allowed HTTP Methods: GET, HEAD, POST, OPTIONS
+ /cgi-sys/formmail.pl: Many versions of FormMail have remote vulnerabilities,
including file access, information disclosure and email abuse. FormMail access
should be restricted as much as possible or a more secure solution found.
+ /cgi-sys/cgiwrap/~bin: cgiwrap can be used to enumerate user accounts. Recompile
cgiwrap with the '--with-quiet-errors' option to stop user enumeration.
+ /cgi-sys/cgiwrap/~daemon: cgiwrap can be used to enumerate user accounts.
Recompile cgiwrap with the '--with-quiet-errors' option to stop user enumeration.
+ /cgi-sys/cgiwrap/~ftp: cgiwrap can be used to enumerate user accounts. Recompile
cgiwrap with the '--with-quiet-errors' option to stop user enumeration.
+ /cgi-sys/cgiwrap/~mysql: cgiwrap can be used to enumerate user accounts.
Recompile cgiwrap with the '--with-quiet-errors' option to stop user enumeration.
+ /cgi-sys/cgiwrap/~operator: cgiwrap can be used to enumerate user accounts.
Recompile cgiwrap with the '--with-quiet-errors' option to stop user enumeration.
+ /cgi-sys/cgiwrap/~root: cgiwrap can be used to enumerate user accounts. Recompile
cgiwrap with the '--with-quiet-errors' option to stop user enumeration.
```

```
+ /cgi-sys/cgiwrap/~sshd: cgiwrap can be used to enumerate user accounts. Recompile
cgiwrap with the '--with-quiet-errors' option to stop user enumeration.
+ /cgi-sys/cgiwrap/~uucp: cgiwrap can be used to enumerate user accounts. Recompile
cgiwrap with the '--with-quiet-errors' option to stop user enumeration.
+ /cgi-sys/cgiwrap/~www: cgiwrap can be used to enumerate user accounts. Recompile
cgiwrap with the '--with-quiet-errors' option to stop user enumeration.
+ /cgi-sys/cgiwrap/~OYG3G: Based on error message, cgiwrap can likely be used to
find valid user accounts. Recompile cgiwrap with the '--with-quiet-errors' option
to stop user enumeration.
+ /cgi-sys/cgiwrap/~root: cgiwrap can be used to enumerate user accounts. Recompile
cgiwrap with the '--with-quiet-errors' option to stop user enumeration.
+ /cgi-sys/cgiwrap: Some versions of cgiwrap allow anyone to execute commands
remotely.
+ /cgi-sys/Count.cgi: This may allow attackers to execute arbitrary commands on the
server
+ OSVDB-3092: /readme.txt: This might be interesting...
+ OSVDB-3093: /cgi-sys/counter-ord: This might be interesting... has been seen in
web logs from an unknown scanner.
+ OSVDB-3093: /cgi-sys/counterbanner: This might be interesting... has been seen in
web logs from an unknown scanner.
+ OSVDB-3093: /cgi-sys/counterbanner-ord: This might be interesting... has been
seen in web logs from an unknown scanner.
+ OSVDB-3093: /cgi-sys/counterfiglet-ord: This might be interesting... has been
seen in web logs from an unknown scanner.
+ OSVDB-3093: /cgi-sys/counterfiglet/nc/: This might be interesting... has been
seen in web logs from an unknown scanner.
+ 6474 items checked: 1 error(s) and 22 item(s) reported on remote host
+ End Time:           2012-03-20 13:50:22 (GMT-6) (993 seconds)
---------------------------------------------------------------------
1 host(s) tested
```

> **Note:** Almost every one of these lines represents a possible vulnerability or exploitable code. Using various options you can fine tune nikto to do exactly what you need, including stealth scans, mutation and cookie detection.

Mightier and Mitre-er

Finding a vulnerability is all well and good but what you do with that information is a whole different story. Security professionals will take the scan results of their own web servers and patch, update, remove, repair or do whatever they need to in order to close each vulnerability. The nice folks over at **Mitre.org** operate several databases (http://mitre.org/work/cybersecurity.html) that collect and catalog every known vulnerability you could imagine.

These databases are given scary names like "**Common Weakness Enumeration (CWE)**" and "**Common Vulnerabilities and Exposures" (CVE)**" yet they are fairly simple to operate. These systems are a collection of other tools and data with a search engine built into each database. Each data repository is focused on different aspects of hardware, software, services, system configurations, and compliance requirements.

Looking at the results nikto gave us earlier, you can see near the bottom of the log are the letters **OSVDB** followed by a bunch of numbers. OSVDB stands for the **Open Source Vulnerability Database** located at OSVDB.org. In the log results from nikto the numbers after OSVDB identify a specific type of vulnerability.

Exercises

4.6   Install **netcat** on a Linux virtual machine or use a live Linux CD/DVD to boot up your computer:

sudo apt-get install netcat   [for Debian/Ubuntu family]

or

sudo yum install netcat   [for Red Hat/Fedora family]

4.7   Install nikto on your Linux virtual machine:

sudo apt-get install nikto   [for Debian/Ubuntu family]

or

sudo yum install nikto   [for Red Hat/Fedora family]

4.8   Repeat the experiments above, targeting www.hackerhighschool.org.

Note: Do not try this on any other public or private web server, including your school's. Bad, bad idea.

Browsing Behind Bars: SSL

When the web started to take off, it wasn't long before everyone realized that HTTP in plain text wasn't good for security. The next variation was to apply encryption to it. This came in the form of **Secure Sockets Layer/Transport Layer Security** (**SSL/TLS**, simply called **SSL**), a cryptographic suite encompassing secure ciphers implementing 40 to 128 bit (or more) symmetric key encryption methods. A 40 bit key is not as secure than a 128 bit key, and with specialized hardware, 40 bit is breakable within a reasonable period of time, like during a lunch break (okay, maybe a bit more than that). The 128 bit key will take much longer: cracking it with only brute force will require somewhere between a trillion years and the total age of the universe. A streaming cipher suite like RC4 only offers protection for about the square root of the key space, or half the length of the key; so a 128 bit key offers protection of 64 bits, which can be cracked on a modern PC in relative short time – think days. One thing to remember is that the stronger the key algorithm you use, the longer it will take to encrypt and decrypt code. Use encryption sparingly or only apply as much strength as you need for web surfing.

Along with SSL, an open source version is available called "**OpenSSL**" and can be found at openssl.org. OpenSSL works alongside Transport Layer Security to provide an entire library of cryptographic recipes. OpenSSL is a command line tool with many options to work with. Turn to http://www.openssl.org/docs/apps/openssl.html for all the latest information on the command interface and library updates.

For known HTTPS attacks there are more complex approaches using something called a **known cyphertext attack**. This involves calculating the encryption key by analyzing a large number of messages (over a million) to deduce the key. Along with **cyphertext**, you will find multiple attack methods that are discovered every day.

Applied SSL

You shouldn't rush to try and crack 128 bit encryption. Since SSL just encrypts standard HTTP traffic, if we set up an SSL tunnel, we can query the server just as we did earlier. Creating an SSL tunnel is a snap, especially since there are utilities like **openssl** and **stunnel** made just for the job.

Exercises

4.9   Macs and Linux machines have openssl already installed. Try this command:

> openssl s_client -connect www.hackthissite.org:443

This connection will only stay open a few seconds, but you can run any HTTP command, like:

> GET www.hackthissite.org/pages/index/index.php

4.10 Check to see if stunnel is installed on your Linux machine or on the live CD. If it's not installed, install it. Go ahead and give it a test drive.

4.11 Once it's installed or at least running on your machine, run the command:

```
stunnel
```

This will tell you the location of the configuration file you need to create.

4.12 At that location, create stunnel.conf and enter this text (replace *ssl.enabled.host* with the name of a real SSL server that you want to connect to):

```
client=yes
 verify=0 [psuedo-https]
 accept = 80
 connect = ssl.enabled.host:443
 TIMEOUTclose = 0
```

4.13 Once that's done you start stunnel with this command:

```
stunnel &
```

Stunnel will map your local computer port 80 (default HTTP port) to SSL/TLS port 443 (default SSL port) and uses plain text, so you can open another shell and connect to it using any of the methods listed above, for instance:

```
netcat 127.0.0.1 80      [hit <Enter>]
HEAD / HTTP/1.0           [hit <Enter> twice]
HTTP/1.1 200 OK
 Server: Netscape-Enterprise/4.1
 Date: Fri, 07 Jan 2005 10:32:38 GMT
 Content-type: text/html
 Last-modified: Fri, 07 Jan 2005 05:32:38 GMT
 Content-length: 5437
 Accept-ranges: bytes
 Connection: close
```

Feed Your Head: Fake SSL Certificates

Until now, in this chapter, we've made the assumption that HTTPS encrypted connections are secure. This is not necessarily the case, since SSL relies on web-of-trust model public key certificates, as well as relying on the user to cancel the connection if a security warning is presented.

When a user requests a website over HTTPS, the server will send the user's browser its SSL certificate that is signed by a trusted Certificate Authority (CA). The browser then checks this SSL certificate against its own database of trusted CAs to determine whether the website should be trusted.

If an attacker is doing an ARP spoofing attack on the local network, and an HTTPS connection is started by one of the users on the network, the attacker is able to intercept the request and produce a false SSL certificate to the user claiming that they are the requested site.

Since this SSL certificate has not been signed by a trusted CA, the web browser will display a dialog box warning the user that a possible attack is being carried out. Thanks to the **trust relationship** that users have with their web applications, both internal and external, most users will simply accept any warnings that a web browser displays, ultimately allowing this type of attack to succeed.

At this stage the attacker's machine then acts as a transparent proxy between the user and the real website, decrypting the communications in between and allowing the HTTPS traffic to be analyzed in clear text, enabling usernames, passwords and other sensitive information to be enumerated. This is commonly known as a **Man In The Middle (MITM)** attack.

The Properties of Trust

The whole SSL-thing is designed around trust. The browsers contain certificates which are really just long numbers that serve as keys. When you use SSL, the S in HTTPS, the certificate of the browser is used to check the certificate of the server and see if it's a trustworthy web server. The theory is that if the domain name matches the SSL certificate of the server as the domain that we visited then it's trustworthy. Of course who says it's trustworthy is a whole other problem. It wouldn't be the first time that a criminal infiltrated the certificate authorities and got the keys to fake their own server certificates that your browser then tells you is trustworthy. In another case, a known skeevy organization that was responsible for making spyware paid its way into being a certificate authority and added to all the browsers. So trust is a big deal on the web. It's another way to attack and it's another way that humans badly understand how to protect against it going wrong.

ISECOM spent time researching trust and discovered 10 main properties. You can read more about these properties in the OSSTMM. But basically, these are 10 things that need to be evaluated to have logical (not emotional, gut-feeling) trust:

Our parent organization ISECOM pioneered the field of trust analysis: the study of reasons we trust – and which reasons are actually good ones.

Trust Property			Description
1		Size	The number to be trusted. Must the trust extend to just one or to many? Is the group to be a trusted one which is meant to make collective decision?
2		Symmetry	The vector (direction) of the trust. Trust may be one way (asymmetrical) and defined as to which way the trust must travel or both ways (symmetrical). A person who must also trust you has to consider the reciprocation from breaking the trust.
3		Visibility	The level of transparency of all operational parts and processes of the target and its environment.
4		Subjugation	Also called *control*, the amount of influence over the scope by the operator.
5		Consistency	The historical evidence of compromise or corruption of the target.
6		Integrity	The amount and timely notice of change within the target.
7		Offsets	The *offsets of sufficient assurance* are compensation for the trust giver or punishment for the trust breaker. It is a value placed on the trust with the target.
8		Value	The financial offset for risk, the amount of win or gain for which the risk of putting trust in the target is sufficient to offset the risk of failure in the trust.
9		Components	The number of other elements which currently provide resources for the target either through direct or indirect interactions, similar to Intervention of the Four Point Process.
10		Porosity	The amount of separation between the target and the external environment.

Figure 3.1: *Trust Properties*

Exercises

4.14 Look at Property 8. Do you think **Value** is a valid reason to trust? Do you think it is a GOOD reason to trust? Would you trust someone because they gave you money? And now: Do you use Gmail? Do you trust the company that provides it because it's free?

Employing a Middleman: Proxies

Using Someone Else's Server

A **proxy server** (or just **proxy**) is a middleman in the HTTP transaction process:

- •The client (your browser) sends its request to the proxy;

- •The proxy stops and holds your request, then sends its own request to the web server;

- •The web server (which doesn't even know who you really are) responds to the proxy; and

- •The proxy relays the response back to the client, completing the transaction.

A proxy can be a server on your own network that lets you pass your connection through it. This is handy because it gives you some protection, since the proxy hides your identity and acts as a firewall between you and the rest of the web. But you can also use a proxy server that's out on the Internet, which hides you even better (on-line you can find many lists of publicly available proxies, such as http://tools.rosinstrument.com/proxy/). These **external proxy servers** provide critical access to the outside world for people in countries that censor or cut off their ISP's connections to the Internet.

But, as you might have figured by now, proxy servers are vulnerable to attacks themselves, and can become jumping-off points for launching attacks on other servers. Not to mention that you may be going through one and not even be aware of it – which means **IT'S RECORDING EVERYTHING YOU DO**. This is something you especially want to consider if you use a free public proxy server. There is absolutely no guarantee the owner of that proxy is honest and will not use your username/password or credit card details. Schools and businesses usually have a proxy to enforce their "appropriate use" policies.

Exercises

4.15 Are you behind a proxy? How can you find out?

4.16 If you lived in a country that blocked access to some web sites, could you find external proxies that would let you access them? If so, wouldn't the government also look for them and block them? How might you overcome this?

Using a Local Proxy

You can run a proxy server right on your local computer. It won't change your source IP address (because its address is the same as yours), but it can prevent caching and filter out undesirable content.

Exercise

4.17 Find a piece of software called Privoxy. If you install it, what will it give you? Are you a candidate to use it?

The Onion Router

The Onion Router, or **TOR**, was created to hide your IP address – many times over. When you use the TOR network, your traffic gets encrypted and passed along through a tangle of routers, and eventually emerges ... somewhere. But in theory your traffic can't be traced back to you. In theory. In reality, some things – like using Flash on TOR – has given unsuspecting users bad surprises.

Technically, you could set up TOR yourself, which involves some interesting configuration. We recommend it for the learning experience. However, most of us mere mortals will appreciate the **TOR Browser**, which has all the defaults set for safety, and lets you do all that interesting research in a separate browser.

Exercises

4.18 Who created TOR? Why?

4.19 Find out where you get it. Get it. Open it up and make it work.

HTML Programming: A Brief Introduction

HTML is a set of instructions that explains how information sent from a web server (Apache, IIS) is to be displayed in a browser (Firefox, Opera). It is the heart of the web. The **World Wide Web Consortium (W3C)** is the standards organization governing the workings of HTML.

HTML can do much more than just display data on a web page. It can also provide data entry forms, for server-side processing by a higher level language (Perl, PHP, etc). In a business setting this is where HTML is most useful, but in a hacker setting this is where HTML is most vulnerable.

> **Note:** HTML is supposed to be a standard format across all platforms (browsers and operating systems), yet this isn't always the case. Some browsers read the HTML slightly different than other browsers just as other OS's won't be compatible with other operating systems. Be sure to cross check your HTML code against other types of browsers to ensure it is interpreted correctly and doesn't show up as a pile of gibberish.

Reading HTML

HTML works by using **tags** or **markup.**-Most opening tags, **<h1>**, for instance, must have a closing tag, **</h1>**. Just a few tags have no closing tag, like **
** and **<img>**.-The markup **<h1>** tells the browser where to start and stop displaying a large, bold heading, for example. **Well-formed HTML** has proper opening and closing tags (and follows other rules as well). One factor to consider in coding (writing) HTML is the need to be read by several different platforms.

Take, for example, the code:

```
<html>
<head>
 <title>My Hello World Page</title>
</head>
 <body>
 <h1>Hello World!</h1>
 <p>I'm a new page.</p>
 </body>
 </html>
```

We are telling the browser this is an HTML document with the tag **<html>**, and inside the **<head>** we give it the title "My Hello World Page" with the **<title>** tag. The My Hello World Page tag tells our browser "here's the information to show to the viewer." Finally, the **<h1>** tag tells the browser to display the information in "Heading 1" style, and the **<p>** tag tells the browser "here's a regular paragraph." The tags that have a "/" are the closing tags, which tell the browser to stop displaying the contents as described by the opening tag.

Exercise

4.20 Search the W3C.org website for the HTML standard. Are the HTML5 standards in the same place? Why wouldn't they be?

4.21 Copy the code above and paste it into a text file called **hello.htm**. Open that file in your browser of choice and you should see something similar to this:

Hello World!
I'm a new page.

Viewing HTML Source Code

All browsers contain a way to view the underlying HTML code that generated the web page you are looking at. In most cases, this is the **View Source** option under the **View** menu in your browser. Many browsers will also show source code if you press Control-U or Command-U.

Exercise

4.22 Go to a web page you often visit. View the source code.

Figure 3.2: *View menu*

The results should be something similar to this:

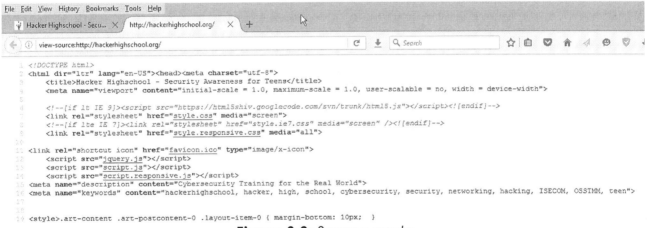

Figure 3.3: *Source code*

HTML code is visible to anyone with a web browser. This is why it is very important, when you create web pages, not to hide passwords or sensitive information in the HTML source code (including comments). As you can see, it's not very secret.

In most browsers you can also view the source by doing a right mouse click and select "view source". The web page can instruct your browser to behave different on a right mouse click. On some sites this is used as a (poor) security measure to prevent visitors from viewing the source. When you select view, view source, it always works on older websites. With some more modern sites, the page source is dynamically and only partially updated. You need additional add ons in Firefox to view such a dynamic source (install the Add-on "Web Developer" in Firefox and the select: View Source, View Generated Source).

Linking Up With Hyperlinks

Links, or **hyperlinks,** are really the heart of HTML. The ability to link from document to document allows you to create **hypertext**, textual knowledge connected to related knowledge. A link, in HTML code, looks like this:

```
<a href="www.yahoo.com">www.yahoo.com</a>
```

This creates a link that looks like www.yahoo.com on your website, and of course will send your visitor away to Yahoo.

Links can be followed and checked by **link checker** programs. These programs search HTML source code for <a href="..."></a> tags and then create a file or index of the links they find. Spammers use this technique to harvest email addresses or identify contact forms they can use to spread their mass emails. Link checkers can also be used to check your website for broken links that don't go anywhere. Due to the dynamic nature of the web, these are depressingly common even in relatively small sites.

Exercises

4.23 Create a link to www.hackerhighschool.org that displays as "Hacker Highschool" on your web page.

4.24 Find and download a link checking program. Run that program against www.hackerhighschool.org and document how many broken links you find.

HTML5

The new flavor of HTML, HTML5, brings a lot of security improvements. It doesn't require Flash to stream videos, which is a huge leap in terms of preventing unwanted tracking and the endless vulnerabilities of Flash.
On the other hand, is carries a whole stack of new problems with it.

Cross Domain Messaging or **Web Messaging** lets HTML5 escape the ugly hacks we've used in HTML4 when documents come from more than one source. The problem is, this kind of messaging requires a lot of trust – and some very secure coding – to ensure nasty things don't get into the middle of this process.

Cross Origin Resource Sharing is when a web server allows its resources to be used by a separate domain. Again, this is a cool way to **mash up** content from multiple sources – but this level of trust just begs to be cracked.

WebSockets provides asynchronous full duplex communication. That's a mouthful, but essentially it means your browser can bypass the usual security measures in return for pure speed.

Local Storage APIs let web pages store data on your computer. Did you know all contemporary browsers include a mini-database called SQLite? Now just ponder: what's stored on your computer in that database? All kinds of interesting things about you, right?

Exercise

4.25 Find an application that lets you look into that SQLite database. Hint: you're looking for a "database browser." Install it and see what's in there!

Scripting Languages

Old-school coding in languages like C++ meant hours of deep coding, then compiling **binaries**, machine-language instructions that run very quickly. If you want raw horsepower, and have a whole lot of time on your hands, this is the world for you.

The rest of us will use **scripting languages** to write **scripts**, programs written in plain text that are interpreted at runtime by binaries (that you don't have to write) underneath. They don't run as fast as freestanding binaries, but with the very fast processors we have today, you may never notice the difference.

Scripting languages are great for dynamic web pages, but they also create a new avenue of attack for hackers. Most web application vulnerabilities aren't caused by bugs in any particular language, but by bad coding and poor web server configuration. For example, if a form requests a zip code but the user enters "abcde", the application should return them to the form and point out the error. This is called **input validation**. Here are some of the most common scripting platforms today:

Common Gateway Interface (CGI): This is the granddaddy of scripting interfaces, and it's not really a language itself; it's a way to run scripts. **Perl** was one of the most popular scripting languages to write CGI programs in the early days, though it's not used much for web pages anymore. Perl is, however, very useful for hackers, and many handy tools are written in this language.

PHP: PHP is a very popular open-source scripting language that runs on the server before the page is sent to the user. The web server uses PHP to get data from databases, respond to user choices and build a dynamic page with the information the visitor wants. HTML displays static content; PHP lets you create pages that give the user dynamic, customized content based on their input. Web pages that contain PHP scripting usually have a file name ending in ".php".

Python: Another popular language, Python is a competitor to PHP, and does many of the same things. Many web sites use both PHP and Python (as well as other languages), including Google.com, Yahoo.com and Amazon.com. Python scripts usually have the file extension .py. In the world of security, you ought to know as much as you can about at least one language. The flavor used today for security pros is Python.

Active Server Pages (ASP): Web pages that have a .asp or .aspx extension (ASPs) are database-driven and dynamically generated just like PHP or Python pages. ASP was Microsoft's first server-side scripting engine for the web. Its popular successor, ASP.NET, is built on the Common Language Runtime (CLR), allowing programmers to write code using any supported .NET language, such as: C#, VB.NET, Jscript.NET, etc. If you love Microsoft you'll love writing code specifically for IIS.

Java Server Pages (JSP): It is a technology that helps software developers create dynamically generated web pages. JSP is similar to PHP, but it uses the Java programming language. To deploy and run, a compatible web server with a servlet container (such as Apache Tomcat) is required.

Coldfusion and **Ruby** have their own cult followings, and there are dozens of less-well-known languages that can do very interesting things.

Javascript: Javascript (which is very much *not* the same thing as Java) probably runs on more web pages than any language besides HTML. It's different from the scripting languages above, because it doesn't run on the server to generate a page. Instead, it runs in your browser after the page arrives. This gives you visual effects like fly-out menus, expandable and collapsible sections of pages and "live" interaction with the page.

Practically every dynamic page uses Javascript somewhere, and it's the front line of defense for validating the information people submit via forms. However, note that client-side input validation only is not enough to guarantee protection against attack targeting dynamic web application parameters. One example of ways to abuse client-side scripting is to pull up a web page, fill in the form, and capture it with a specialized proxy. The proxy lets you rewrite the code in the returned page and send it back using bogus values. You could also do this by "saving" the web page, editing the code, then sending it back using netcat. Or you could simply disable Javascript in your browser, using either built-in controls or add-ons.

Game On: Wireless Friends

Mokoa knew when to keep his mouth shut but Officer Hank was still learning the proper technique around Jace. So the unwitting cop made the error of saying something really stupid to the hacker: "How can we put dynamic content in our web pages, like being able to search for data, or request certain information?"

Her chair was facing the computer monitor so Jace didn't even waste the effort of turning around to answer this question. Hank was behind her, hovering over her slim shoulder as if he could actually read what was being typed on the keyboard. Jace was working in HTML5 and trying to build a Javascript to request a PHP weather-application API widget.

Jace didn't bother to slow down her rapid typing/coding as she let out a huff of arrogant air. "Hank, we already talked about this."

"We did?"

"Yup, I brought up the security concerns of dynamic content so I'll go over cross-site scripting a bit more. Please pay attention this time."

Smart-ass, thought Hank.

"Taking user input and returning it to the user without proper encoding enables cross-site scripting. Cross-site scripting, or XSS, occurs when dynamically generated Web pages display input that is not properly validated or sanitized. This allows an attacker to embed malicious Javascript code into the generated page and execute the script on the machine of any user who views that site.

"Check out what happens when I enter this text into the search field on a search engine whose value will be displayed on the page after it is posted back."

She typed in:

<script>alert('Vulnerable')</script>

"Do you see a pop-up message box with the message 'Vulnerable?' That page is vulnerable to cross-site scripting. An attacker who uses cross-site scripting can compromise confidential information, manipulate or steal cookies, create requests that can be mistaken for those of a valid user or execute malicious code on end-user systems. We don't want that, do we," Jace asked.

Hank looked a little sick but asked anyways, "Can we fix this?"

Jace laughed a bit and answered, "We can, by passing all user input through the Server.HTMLEncode() function. This takes the users input and checks to make sure it is legit before it is sent to the Javascript or PHP script for execution, depending on whether it's happening client-side or server-side."

Mokoa and Hank looked at each other to see if either had a clue about what Jace just said. They both shrugged. Jace kept banging away on the keyboard, fully aware that her two sidekicks didn't understand what she was talking about.

"Dude, I need a soda. Can one of you get me a refreshing drink to cool my parched lips? All this work is making me thirsty," Jace fluttered her eyelashes in the direction of the police officer. "Oh, can you get one for Mokoa too?" The remark was obviously aimed at Hank, since he was the only one who could get to the police station vending machine and back without raising suspicions.

Hank reached into his deep pant pockets. He pulled out his keys; a pack of gum, some mints, a toothpick, a USB thumb drive, a half used pack of aspirin, two wads of pocket lint, and some small change.

Mokoa replied, "The machine takes credit cards. Could you make my drink water?"

Officer Hank grunted, showing his displeasure at being their errand boy to fetch drinks. He did owe them both more than a soda for their time and effort but he didn't have to like it.

Jace waited a few seconds after Hank left before she started talking again, "See, here's the problem. Someone in this building did a back-up of the web site and stored that back-up in a publicly accessible directory. All the attacker had to do was search for this type of file, download it, and then they could see all the passwords inside the actual web site. These services were shut off when I finished last week. I don't let any unnecessary services like debug, custom error messages, or those types of programs operate if I'm not on the console."

Mokoa asked the question, "So who and how did the police get into the web server?"

Jace bit her lip and tried to think of a good answer. It wasn't Jace's fault that the police web site was attacked. But, then again, the police didn't seem smart enough to know how to hack the set up she'd created. How and why did another cop gain access to the web site? The questions troubled Jace.

Hank came back empty handed. The soda machine was out of order. The police officer said that he was heading home for the night anyways.

Officer Hank gave Jace a tough squeeze hug with one arm while shaking Mokoa's hand with the other. Once the goodbyes were finished, he headed back out the small office door, explaining that he was going home for dinner to the wife and kids. With a final quick wink to Mokoa, the police officer was gone.

The two teens stood looking at each other for a moment before Jace mocked, "'I think she likes you.' Why didn't you say anything back?"

Mokoa didn't seem to care about her allegations. "He was only joking. You gotta relax once in a while. Not everyone is out to get you. You DO have a few friends left."

Mokoa almost heard a click sound from Jace, like a clock tick or a lock being opened miles away. It was the lightest of sounds yet so familiar that he knew instinctively where to look for the reason. He turned to face Jace.

Jace scrambled to open up her satchel. Without explanation she pulled out her cellphone and pressed her slender fingers over the screen. A WiFi analyzer came to life on her phone and began to scan the airwaves.

"What?" Mokoa asked, slightly fearing her answer.

"Mokoa, what you just said made me remember something. You said, 'Not everyone is out to get me,' and something about having friends. How would you keep in contact with a friend?" She asked.

"I would call them or text them, I guess. Why?" he answered back.

The cellphone application displayed several WiFi devices in the area. Mokoa couldn't see the screen but did see the reaction on Jace's face. She began looking around, trying to act normal, trying not to act suspicious. Putting her phone face down on the desk she said, "I gotta go to the bathroom."

Game continues...

Web Vulnerabilities

Giving someone what they ask for is simple; selling them something is a lot less simple. Online stores, companies selling products, bloggers selling ideas and personality, or newspapers selling news – all require more than just HTML-encoded text and pictures. Dynamic web sites that market products based on your preferences, show you alternatives, recommend other options, up-sell add-ons and make sure you pay for what you get require complex software. They're no longer static web sites, they're web applications. When we say goodbye to web sites and hello to web applications, we enter a whole new world of security issues.

Lions, Tigers and Bears Oh My!

We mentioned earlier "complexity breeds insecurity". Now we are going to look at the true meaning behind that mantra. When the automobile was first invented, it was nothing more than a wheel, one simple wheel. Some folks thought that the wheel was just fine but other people wanted to improve on that wheel. These early hackers began to add more wheels together attached with an axle and a frame. Others added seats to the frame and still more added a fancy horn or installed a horse as the engine. As time went on, this simple wheel automobile slowly took shape into a fast multi-horse drawn carriage. Luckily, someone added a brake before too many other got hurt. Today, we have airbags, seat belts, V-8 engines, and really great sound systems in our cars without having to smell horse dung all the time.

The Internet's evolution has progressed in a similar fashion. People weren't happy staring at a green display screen so they added a color monitor. The old dreary ASCII text became flashing lights and splash colors with midi sounds giving way to 3-D surround sound. Each new upgrade to the Internet added a new level of complexity, another layer of vulnerabilities to consider.

Let's take a ride on the Vulnerability Train to see some of the threats in their natural habitat.

SQL Injection - The Lion

A **SQL injection** isn't so much as an attack against a web site but rather an attack to gain access to databases behind the web site. The primary purpose of a SQL injection is to bypass the web pages. An attacker will want to gain either super user privileges to the databases associated with the web site or get the web page to dump database information into the attacker's hands.

SQL is the basic building block for databases. SQL commands will perform whatever task it is asked, including giving up passwords, credit card numbers, and so forth. All the attacker is doing is adding rogue SQL code (injecting) to any open form field on a web page.

For example, a web page asks a user if they would like to sign up for a monthly newsletter. The page will have open fields for the user to enter their name, email address, and whatever else the web builder wants. Each open field allows a user to input text, which is then stored in a database. A SQL injection simply requires an attacker to input SQL commands into the open fields. If the open fields are not protected (parsed) against allowing such commands, the attacker can easily type a request into an open field for a password list.

Here is an example of such a SQL request that has been slightly sanitized for your protection.

```php
<?php
$query  = "SELECT '1', concat(uname||'-'||passwd) as name, '1971-01-01', '0'
from usertable;
        WHERE size = '$size'";
$result = odbc_exec($conn, $query);

?>
```

SQL injections are the most popular form of attack vectors. This attack can be rendered useless by correctly filtering SQL escape characters in user input fields or building your web site without using SQL. Don't forget about the URL field, that's a user input field too! Not to mention HTTP headers, cookies and more.

Buffer Overflows - The Tiger

Think of a buffer as a small cup. This buffer cup holds a certain amount of data and will spill if too much data is added. When the buffer cup overflows, because someone or something tried to add too much data, the system behaves strangely. When a system behaves strangely, other weird things can happen. A **buffer overflow** is an attack (or accident) where too much data is forced into a buffer that was only built for a certain amount or type of data.

When we look to the same open fields used in SQL injections, we can insert massive amounts of gibberish into fields that were designed to handle 25 characters. What happens when we add 1 million characters to that same field? The web page goes a little crazy and can provide an entry point to an attacker.

Buffer overflows can be avoided by limiting the amount of acceptable data to each open field and ensuring rogue code/commands can't be run inside these user input fields.

Cross Site Scripting (XSS) - The Bear

Our first two vulnerabilities were direct attacks against a server. **Cross Site Scripting (XSS)** is a client side vulnerability that exploits a user's trust to gain access into the web servers the client is looking at. A good example of this type of attack is when an attacker hitch hikes on a users browser while that user is logged in to a security site, such as a bank. The attacker preys on the users established trust between the user and the bank to gain access.

The attacker has various methods to piggy-back on users browsers. Some attackers will establish a **Phishing** web site or create a web site that looks identical to the one the user would visit. Since few people pay any attention to the URL field in their browser, it is fairly common for an attacker to lure a victim into allowing malware to be installed in their browser. Email is the preferred method to install malware since humans are, well, human. Java is another application that can be used to install malware from a malicious web site.

The attacker uses the trust of that user when they log onto an HTTPS site or any useful site the attacker would like to gain entrance into. One method you can use to protect yourself against this type of attack is to keep your browser updated and disable scripting in the browser "options". Based on your type of browser, there are add-ons available that can eliminate URL redirecting and stop any script that may appear dangerous.

Exercise

4.26 Go to http://scriptalert1.com/. Set up at least one tool from that page. Be prepared to explain what it does, how it's installed or set up and what security issue it addresses.

Feed Your Head: Cross Site Scripting (XSS) In Depth

Reflected XSS

Reflected XSS occurs when client-supplied data is echoed back to the end user without being validated or **sanitized** properly by the web application. In this context sanitizing means "taking the magic" out of characters that have special meaning in code; the special meaning of that character is removed. For example, good code should convert the **<**-character in any submission into **<** or **<**. The code function of the character is gone, but the browser will display a **<**.

If client-supplied data is insufficiently validated/sanitized, an attacker may be able to inject HTML or Javascript code into a web parameter, causing the web application to echo this code back to the end user. This injected code is then interpreted and executed by the user's web browser. Oops.

This vulnerability can be used to alter the look of the vulnerable web page, or to trick a user into running malicious Javascript code, including capturing session identifiers or performing Javascript port scanning against an internal network. The following code listing demonstrates how an attacker can inject malicious Javascript into a vulnerable web application parameter, which when echoed back to the user will rewrite the entire web page. This code listing relies on the browser supporting the document.clear() and document.write() Javascript functions.

```
http://www.organization.com/?vulnparam=<IMG
SRC=`Javascript:document.clear();document.write("XSS")`>
```

This attack causes the actual URL for the organization's web application to be displayed within the address bar of the victim's web browser even though the entire contents of the page have been rewritten. The attacker exploits the trust relationship that the user has with the URL when they see the correct domain name shown in the address bar of their browser. This may stop some users from becoming suspicious about entering their details into the malicious web page.

Stored XSS

Stored XSS (or Persistent XSS) is slightly different, since instead of the client-supplied data being echoed back to the end user immediately, the data is stored on the server and is sent to the user each time the page is requested. This is common when posting messages on web forums, where the user's message is stored on the server and is sent back to any user who opens the message. If the data contained within the user's message is not validated properly by the web application, an attacker may be able to inject malicious Javascript code into the message that will be run by every user who views the message.

This type of attack can be used to deface a website by permanently rewriting the vulnerable page, or can be used to perform session hijacking attacks by injecting Javascript that sends session identifiers to the attacker each time a user visits the page. The latter attack may compromise the account of every user that views the vulnerable page.

Cross-Site Request Forgery

Cross-Site Request Forgery, or Session Riding, is an interesting vulnerability that allows an attacker to exploit a user who is already authenticated to a web application, and tricks the user into performing authenticated actions, usually without them even knowing.

A great example of this vulnerability is when a user has authenticated to their web mail service and an attacker has sent the user an email containing a link that changes their password. This attack does not necessarily rely on the user clicking the link, or even seeing the link. If the link is embedded within an IMG tag in an HTML email then the action will be carried out automatically when the browser attempts to load the image, as shown by the following IMG tag.

```
<img src=http://www.orgwebmail.com/passwd.php?new=hacked width=0
height=0>
```

A Cross-Site Request Forgery can also be carried out via Stored XSS attacks, causing any user visiting the page to automatically have their password changed via the link in the injected IMG tag. Then the attacker simply logs in to each of the users' accounts with the newly set passwords.

If web application sessions do not timeout when browsing away from the application, an attacker may be able to lure the user into visiting a malicious website that includes a malicious IMG tag that could immediately take advantage of the still-authenticated session.

Cross-Site Request Forgery can have much greater consequences depending upon the value of the web application being attacked. A hacker may be able to force an authenticated Internet banking user into transferring funds from their account into the attacker's account without even knowing that it has been done.

This attack assumes that the hacker knows the internal web application URL for the desired action, such as the exact URL to transfer funds from one account to another, and that the user's web browser will send the session identifiers to the web application when the link is visited.

If the attacker has their own account for the target web application, or is able to download and setup their own copy of the web application, then the first assumption above isn't too difficult to overcome.

The second assumption may require the same web browser instance to make the request to the web application so that the session identifiers are transmitted automatically. This is highly probable in the situation where the user is viewing the malicious email within their web mail service, or where the user has browsed away from their web application to visit a malicious site. However, if the user is reading the email from within a software based email program and needs to click on a link within the email, then this link is likely to be opened in a new web browser window that will not have the web application session details.

Bear Traps and Tiger Rugs

Each web application event and every web site you visit can bring potential harm to you or your loved ones. This doesn't mean that you should unplug from the Internet and go back to crayons in some remote cave somewhere. Each minute of each day new threats are presented and some are more successful than others. However, as a security professional, it is (or will be) your job to learn as much as you can about emerging threats and how to protect against them.

Honey pots can be used to lure bad guys into exposing themselves or track them as they probe your network. It is also common practice to apply maximum security and privacy settings to your firewall. You are using a firewall, aren't you? If you are not using a firewall, stop reading immediately and install a firewall this very instant. Once installed, max out the security and privacy settings. Your network router can be used as a firewall, as you should use both hardware and software firewalls. Don't forget the malware protection software (anti-virus).

Next on the list of self preservation is using anomaly detection software, otherwise know as **Intrusion Detection Systems (IDS).** An IDS can be as simple as a program running in the computer's background that looks for changes to system files. More sophisticated IDS's will perform more sophisticated actions, like sounding alarms or rerouting an ongoing attacker into a honey pot. We'll talk more about these later on.

Some often overlooked aspects of security is cyber law knowledge, compliance requirements, auditing, and knowing what government regulations you need to adhere to. Yes, those do sound lame but having a basic understanding of these areas can prevent you from making the international news headlines. Jurisdiction is a constant problem when an attacker is based in another country. Knowing what you can do and what you can't do to pursue an attacker is valuable information.

Exercises

4.27 What can happen if a web application doesn't perform validation on the data that the user inputs?

4.28 What are Cross-Site Scripting (XSS) and SQL injection? How does an attacker use them to steal data or gain access?

4.29 What security and privacy settings do you have on your own system? What about the rest of your family's computers?

4.30 Look up at least two different methods to mitigate SQL injections and describe them as a feasible addition to a web host. Tell us what they mean and how they work.

4.31 Do a Google search on the terms "inurl:search.asp" or "inurl:search.php". How many results do you get?

4.32 Find a search form at www.hackthissite.org, and type in:

<script>alert ("hello")</script>

What happens?

Now, think: what happens if you try this on other sites? What kind of peril are you in if you do this?

4.33 Do a Google search on the terms "inurl:login.asp" and "inurl:login.php". Once again, consider how web sites invite attack simply by using these names.

4.34 Back on www.hackthissite.org, find a login form and attempt to type in special characters (@#$^&) for both the username and password. What happens? Do you think this kind of probing is logged?

Using a Local Proxy for Web Application Testing

An external proxy isn't the only kind of proxy server. You can also install a proxy server right onto your own computer, where it can perform some of the same firewall and filtering functions as an external proxy. Proxies designed specifically for testing web applications can manipulate data requests to test how the web server will respond. That means that with a proxy testing utility (such as Burp Suite, SpikeProxy etc.), you can run various cross-site scripting attacks, SQL injection attacks and almost any other direct request attack. While some of these proxy server utilities have an automation feature, the best tester is a real person behind the keyboard.

Remember, these tools are designed for you to test your own web applications! Be sure to test only websites for which you have permission, or you will most certainly be logged, and possibly jailed.

Exercises

4.35 Find and download **Burp Suite**. How do you install it? How do you run it?

4.36 Change your browser settings to point to the new proxy. This is usually localhost port 8080, but since these tools may be updated read the instructions to be sure. (Tip: the IP address 127.0.0.1 is the localhost address.)

4.37 Pull down the Help menu and select User Guide. Take a look at the documentation.

4.38 Now spend some time browsing the web site you're testing, in this case www.hackerhighschool.org. Test out forms and visit every page. You're creating a recording, so try to be thorough!

4.39 Once you have surfed around with your browser, go back to the ZAP interface and save your session.

4.40 Right-click on the www.hackerhighschool.org listing on the left, and note the types of attacks you can run. Try them.

A proxy server can be a powerful tool in helping you determine how solid a web application is. For penetration tests or vulnerability assessments, a proxy utility is a good tool in your toolbox. But it's not the only one.

Looking Behind the Curtains

There is a lot going on that's not visible when you request a web page. Long before a page loads, **headers** and **cookies** are flying back and forth, and if you know how, you can see them.

Cookies are usually harmless, and only hold things like a unique user ID, so that when you visit that famous online retailer, the site already knows who you are and what you like.

Figure 3.4 *Cookies*

HTTP headers can be confusing. HTTP is Hyper Text Transfer Protocol: notice the **P**! It's a transmission protocol, a way to send signals down the wire.

Headers get transmitted invisibly with every web request, and usually you never see them. Here's what they look like:

```
http://en-us.fxfeeds.mozilla.com/en-US/firefox/headlines.xml
GET /en-US/firefox/headlines.xml HTTP/1.1
Host: en-us.fxfeeds.mozilla.com
User-Agent: Mozilla/5.0 (Macintosh; Intel Mac OS X 10.7; rv:11.0)
Gecko/20100101 Firefox/11.0
Accept: text/html,application/xhtml+xml,application/xml;q=0.9,*/*;q=0.8
Accept-Language: en-us,en;q=0.5
Accept-Encoding: gzip, deflate
Connection: keep-alive
X-Moz: livebookmarks
HTTP/1.1 302 Found
Content-Encoding: gzip
Cache-Control: max-age=604800
Content-Type: text/html; charset=iso-8859-1
Date: Fri, 23 Mar 2012 00:50:26 GMT
Expires: Fri, 30 Mar 2012 00:50:26 GMT
Last-Modified: Sun, 18 Mar 2012 10:39:59 GMT
```

```
Location: http://fxfeeds.mozilla.com/firefox/headlines.xml
Server: ECS (lax/2872)
Vary: Accept-Encoding
X-Backend-Server: pm-web01
X-Cache: 302-HIT
X-Cache-Info: cached, cached
Content-Length: 200
-----------------------------------------------------------
http://fxfeeds.mozilla.com/firefox/headlines.xml
GET /firefox/headlines.xml HTTP/1.1
Host: fxfeeds.mozilla.com
User-Agent: Mozilla/5.0 (Macintosh; Intel Mac OS X 10.7; rv:11.0)
Gecko/20100101 Firefox/11.0
Accept: text/html,application/xhtml+xml,application/xml;q=0.9,*/*;q=0.8
Accept-Language: en-us,en;q=0.5
Accept-Encoding: gzip, deflate
Connection: keep-alive
```
[and many more...]

The HTML programming language (notice the **L**!) has a part of the document called the **<head>**, but that is *not* the same thing; it's where hidden things like scripts or meta tags go.

Even worse, HTML has **headings**: <h1>, <h2> etc. These are yet a third thing, bold headings for documents! We apologize for the confusion, but you do have to understand the difference.

So when we're talking about HTTP headers, we're talking about the hidden, behind-the-scenes chatter that happens before your page is even sent.

You can use tools like the Firefox add-ons **Live HTTP Headers** and **TamperData** to capture headers, which gets you a display like this:

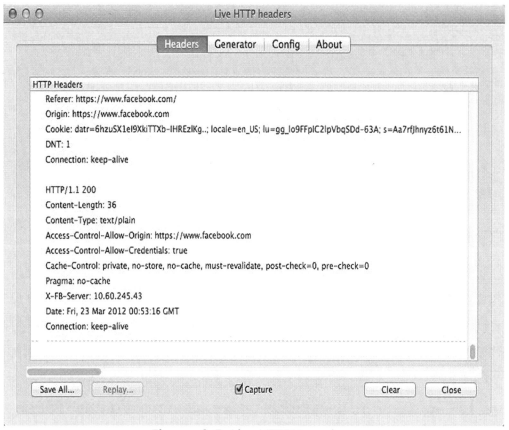

Figure 3.5: *LiveHTTPHeaders*

You can use other tools, like **Add N Edit Cookies** or the **Web Developer** add-on, to capture the cookie information your browser is exchanging with the web site you're visiting. Notice that you can also edit that information. Finally, local proxies can also be used to intercept, analyze and modify cookies.

Exercises

4.41 Find and install the LiveHTTPHeaders add-on for Firefox. How do you use it?

4.42 Find and install the Web Developer add-on as well. How do you use it to view and edit cookies?

4.43 If you think a web application uses the User-Agent for some purpose (why do they care what browser you're using?), check what happens if you remove it. Most applications don't anticipate a missing User-Agent, so when they inspect the content, they're referring to a missing variable. In most cases the application throws an unhandled "object not set" exception, which can include stack dumps or even source code snippets (for instance, with .Net apps with the debugging option on). Sometimes this gives very interesting results.

Game On: Analyzing the Loot

Even though her bedroom window was small, the sun managed to glare off her screen and shine directly in the hacker's eyes where she sat at her cluttered computer desk. Calling this crappy table her "desk" was an insult to any furniture on four legs, but it was the only thing she could afford to hold up her computer. She picked at a loose edge of duct tape, chuckling at the irony of how nicely it color coordinated with her bedroom. Her room was hot but turbulent: the ceiling fan moved the air around with enough force to at least make sweating useful.

The same ceiling fan that her grandfather accidentally tossed Jace into when they were playing years ago. Young Jace only suffered a bump on her porcelain forehead but Grandpa suffered the wrath of both Sweet G and Oace, her mother. That was a long time ago but the fan blades still made a funny whomping sound as they spun.

The computer screen was split into two panels. The left side of the screen showed Metasploit, the right side Wireshark running. Jace was focused on the right portion of the monitor since it was decoding the IP packets she'd captured a few days ago. There weren't any finger smudges on that side of the screen either. Dust poofed when the sunlight made her sneeze.

Jace had spent a few hours hanging out at the burger joint around the corner from the telecommunication company's building. She'd used her old laptop to capture all the WiFi traffic in range. The lunch spot was a popular location for the telcom employees because of exactly that free WiFi access.

Since the food place was packed at lunch and almost everyone worked for the telecom giant, at least half the people in the place were checking on both work and home email while they ate. Jace snickered and munched on french fries, grabbing gigs of IP traffic.

She was running Tails to cover her tracks. The teen also liked using a local small college as her initial proxy. Dinky schools don't have trained staff to audit their logs properly. Even if the education server was audited, her activities would show up as coming from several anonymous sources because she was using Tor and Onion routing in Tails.

Tails protected her identity, spoofed her MAC, redirected all packet requests, hid her real IP address and used Onion Tor to throw off any deep audits. Because she was also starting her hack from the hamburger restaurant's own open access point, she needed additional cover to protect her identity, so Jace used Privoxy as her second launch point. Privoxy doesn't cache any user data; she'd read how privacy advocates used it to protect their identities. It was a nice setup as long as she was close to the WiFi access point. Distance slowed things down.

Meanwhile she put her cellphone in her shirt pocket, camera lens facing out, recording people keying screens around her. Credentials are always handy.

She brought home a USB drive full of packet captures. Now Wireshark was searching for packets holding logon requests, credentials, passwords, user names, user IP addresses, user MAC addresses and anything valuable. Jace had exactly what she needed in her hunt for access to the telecom web servers.

Game continues...

Building Secure Web Applications

Have you ever considered building a web site? Selling something online? Building a web community? In some ways, it's getting simpler all the time. But in terms of security, it just keeps getting trickier.

Secure programming starts with the programmers. Each has his or her own logic and skills with particular languages. But there are accepted guidelines that a programmer determined to write secure code can follow, like the ones derived from the OSSTMM (**http://osstmm.org**):

1. Security should not require user decisions.

2. Every input and output in the application should have a business justification.

3. Quarantine and validate all inputs including the application's own content. Most especially, re-validate **_all_** the data server-side. Someone, somewhere, will try the trick of sending you bad data.

4. Tightly limit the systems and users the application trusts.

5. Encrypt data stored and in transit.

6. Create hashes of all the application's files, so you can check for unauthorized changes.

7. Make sure that all interactions occur on the server side.

8. Layer the security.

9. Invisibility is the best defense. Show only the service itself.

10. Build in triggers for alarms.

11. Promote security awareness in users and technical support people.

Exercises

4.44 What kind of error messages have you seen online? Do you remember where you got them, or how? Could you do it again?

4.45 Name three ways you could build an alarm into a web application.

Protecting Your Server

Consider what it's like to run your own server. You can set it up to do anything you like. Interested in Java or PHP? Joomla or OpenWiki? Photography, animals or both? That's the upside. The downside is that unethical people will try to do unethical things to your server.

You'll have to take some steps to protect your server. These include ensuring that your OS software is always up-to-date with patches, updates and service packs. And do the same thing with your web server software, your database software, your firewall, your antivirus, your intrusion detecting system, all of your installed software (which makes a good point: the less you install, the better!). There are many sources for correct configuration of servers (also called **hardening**), scattered around the Web. If you are running a server, search for those sources and read through some of them.

Firewalls

Firewalls originally were fireproof walls in a building or used between your car engine and the occupants (old school stuff). We use the same words for systems (either hardware and software) that are designed to prevent unauthorized access to a network. Just as a firewall in a building can be a matter of life and death, network firewalls are critical to the health and survival of computer systems.

The key to understanding firewalls is that they're based on sets of **rules**, commonly called **ACLs (Access Control Lists)**. Imagine the rules for a security guard at a school: anyone with a school ID can enter, but no one else can; anyone can exit, except that small children have to be with a parent. The rules for a network firewall are very similar, for instance:

1. Nobody from the Internet gets to come in, except by invitation.

2. Anybody from inside the network can go out to the web, except when this poses a risk.

Simple as that! (If only it were.) In the digital world, we have to work with three things: MACs, IP addresses, and port numbers. You're familiar with ports and protocols from Lesson 3. Here's where you can use this information: if you're running a web server, you need to open port 80 to allow HTTP traffic. If you've got a secure website, you'll need to open port 443. *But only these ports.* Anything else is an open invitation to attackers.

Also, unlike a security guard, a pure network firewall basically isn't very smart. It doesn't look inside of packets, so it can't tell what's being transmitted. That means you could do clever things like paste the contents of corporate documents into forms on a convenient website, and steal intellectual property.

At least, you used to be able to do things like that. The newest generation of "**smart firewalls**" (which are actually very, very smart proxy servers) can indeed tell exactly what's in every IP packet. Woe unto you if you try to sneak a stolen credit card number past this kind of system, because you will be not just detected but identified.

Which brings us to the subject of intrusion detection.

Intrusion Detection Systems/Intrusion Prevention Systems

Let's return to our school. It has good security guards at the doors and gates, but they could be fooled by a fake ID (and yes, you can fake or **spoof** your IP address). Also, the guards go home at night. We need another line of defense, in case somebody who shouldn't have access slips in: we need burglar alarms.

Intrusion Detection Systems (IDSs) are our alarm systems. They can detect the burglar, as well as call the police and ring a loud bell. In the Internet world this means noticing abnormal activity, realizing that something is wrong and sending email and text alerts.

Newer systems include **Intrusion Prevention Systems (IPSs)**, which are even more active: if an attack is detected, they can cut off traffic, block IP addresses and even launch countermeasures.

Exercises

4.46 What was the original popular IDS? What is its nickname?

4.47 If you had to pay a lot of money for either one, would you want your server to have a firewall, an IDS/IPS or both?

 Game On: Obsessive Compulsive

One of the tools Jace depended on is Nmap. She had run a series of scans against the telcom in the past. One thing she was able to find out using

```
nmap ipaddress -O --osscan-guess
```

was that certain hardware on the network was Cisco stuff. A little web searching verified that the telcom had upgraded their security appliances to Cisco's All-in-one Next Generation Firewall, IPS and VPN products. Jace checked this by using a program called Burp. Even though it has that funny name, it's a serious tool for web app security testing.

With Burp, the teen hacker built a custom proxy listener with redirection and invisible

---

proxying to inspect the Adaptive Security Device Manager (ASDM) HTTPS transport layer traffic of the telcom's SSL VPN. She used the login credentials from a user she'd already grabbed from the packet capturing session. Redirection allowed the binding of local ports to remote ports on the secure server. Invisible proxying is nothing but a transparent proxy to allow for hidden snooping inside the network. She'd been studying hard at http://portswigger.net/burp/help/suite_gettingstarted.html.

All this means is Burp is an excellent tool to fingerprint web applications and devices. Since firewalls are part of web networks, they can be detected and identified just like an operating system can be. Burp showed Jace that this particular SSL VPN was running on a Cisco ASA 5500 device.

Cisco Adaptive Security Appliance operating system runs on all ASA 5500 series firewalls and VPN appliances. Once she knew this, Jace headed over to http://cve.mitre.org to see what vulnerabilities could be used to help her against these devices. From its Internet connections, she found three different SSL VPNs for the telcom, each running WebVPN as a clientless connection.

CVE-2014-2127 is a vulnerability published by a team of married researchers, Laura Guay and Johnathan Claudius, back in April 2014. This exploit allows an authenticated user on a clientless SSL VPN to elevate their privileges to admin on that network. Of course, having admin rights on any network means having access to lots of other services and areas a typical user can't touch. Every hacker in the world wants admin rights and Jace did too, just as she knew that attempting to get them is against the law.

The sun glared off her monitor and bounced painfully into her hazel eyes. She turned the monitor one direction and then another but the sun was determined to blind her. Frustrated, Jace moved her chair around to the other side of her weird desk. All that did was make the sun shine from her bedroom window directly into her eyes. The teen rubber them and decided she needed a cookie break in the kitchen. The desk wobbled alarmingly as she stood up to leave her computer.

Caught by surprise, her grandmother, Sweet G, was standing in her bedroom doorway. Jace was startled to see her elder leaning against the doorframe.

Sweet G said in a quiet voice, "I'm sorry darling, I didn't mean to sneak up on you. You've been in here all locked up since this morning. I was worried." Grandma carried that soft smile on her face that could have meant anything to Jace. The teen wasn't sure if she was in trouble or that her grandmother was actually concerned about her solitude.

Jace twisted the monitor away from the door to face the bedroom back wall. She replied, "I'm sorry G. I guess time got away from me. What did I miss? How are you doing?"

Sweet G answered back in a calm voice, "Honey, it is 7 pm. You missed breakfast, lunch and now dinner and we live in a very small apartment. I called for you several times to come and eat but all I could hear from you was typing and a few swear words. What have you been doing all this time?"

After looking down at her feet, Jace innocently replied that she was doing school work. She explained that it was a huge project that was due the next day.

Grandma folded her arms and said, "Jace, if that is what you want me to believe than that is fine. But today is Saturday. I'm no fool. I may be old but I'm not stupid. You've been hacking, haven't you?" Sweet G's eyes doubled in size behind her thick glasses as her concerned expression turned to disappointment.

Game Over

Secure Communications

What do we mean by "secure communications" on the web? The phrase sounds like something you'd hear in a spy movie, but actually it's critical to a lot of things we do online. Communicating securely requires a lot of **PAIN**: **Privacy** (and **confidentiality**), **authentication**, **integrity** and **non-repudiation**.

Consider your account at that really famous social network. Obviously, you have to have a user name and password so you can log in to the account. And there are all kinds of privacy settings you can tweak, especially about who can see your most private stuff, so you really don't want anybody else getting into it. Which means you're counting on **authentication** to give you some security. So, does authenticating yourself to the web site makes you safe?

No.

You might be completely deceived about the web site. Someone could send you a **phishing** email that looks exactly like a notice from that social network. Click that link, and it looks like you've gone to the site, but you've actually gone to a malicious site and gotten yourself infected with malware. Or you might make a simple mistake, like typing **whitehouse.com** instead of **whitehouse.gov** – and ending up at a porn site. (No, it's not there any more! But do check out **http://www.antiphishing.org.**)

This means authentication is a two-way street. You should have to identify yourself, certainly. But the site should provide authentication credentials too, and on the web, they come in the form of a **certificate.** When you go to a famous web retailer, and buy products online, your browser probably accepts the web site's certificate automatically, because it comes from one of the big-name, big-dollar certificate authorities like **Verisign.**

When you go to a less famous site, you may be prompted by your browser to accept or refuse its certificate. There is no more critical time on the web to read the details carefully! If you know you want to shop there, then perhaps you should accept the certificate. But if you have no idea why you're being asked to accept a certificate, then you probably shouldn't take it. The idea to understand is that a site's certificate provides its identification and authentication. You're trusting that ID.

So you've ordered that book (or whatever). You don't want the price changed after you order, naturally, or the number of books. And the retail website doesn't want anyone altering critical details like your credit card number. What you both want is **integrity**, which means that what you communicated hasn't been changed.

This is really critical when it comes to big-money transactions. No one should be able to change the dollar amount in the document you send to make an offer for a house – at least not without detection. And the way you do that is by having your computer calculate a **hash** from that offer document. A hash is the result of some complex math, but basically it's a big number that will be unique for every document.

On any Unix computer (which includes Linux and Macintosh), you can calculate an **MD5 hash** (that's the most common kind, although it's not considered that secure anymore and is therefore slowly being replaced by SHA-1, SHA-256 and similar algorithms) with a simple command. Let's say your letter is named Offer.txt. In a shell you can use the following command:

```
md5 Offer.txt
```

and you'll get back something like:

```
MD5 (Offer.txt) = d41d8cd98f00b204e9800998ecf8427e
```

The long string of numbers and letters (actually, it's a **hexadecimal** or **hex** number) is the hash. If someone changed so much as one period in that document, the hash would be totally different. Oh, so the hash you made before you sent the document no longer matches the document's hash now? Watch out! The document has been changed! And you might be buying a much more expensive house if you're not careful.

It's not just you that has to do the trusting in our real estate transaction. The people you send your letter to need to be certain you can't say, "I never sent that offer!" What they want is **non-repudiation**, which means that you can't deny making the offer. And if they accept your offer, you don't want them to repudiate their acceptance later. So how can we make sure of this?

Hashing does the trick here as well, though the process is more complex. You learned in another lesson about getting yourself a PGP/GPG key pair, which you can then use to create a **signature.** A signature works here because nobody but you can create that signature – and it will be different for every document you sign. At its root, that signature is just another hash.

Privacy and Confidentiality

Privacy means keeping your information yours, or at least maintaining control over it. This may be as simple as protecting your credit card number, or as complicated as keeping your new love affair secret.

What you do on the web stays private, right? You know by now that's not true. Web sites gather information about you constantly, particularly the search engine giants. You sign away your privacy when you accept that free email account, or when you join a social network. Web sites that collect information are supposed to have a **privacy policy** that clearly spells out how they will use your information. If you visit a site that wants information but doesn't have a privacy policy, *get out!*

When you visit, sites set **cookies** on your computer. Cookies aren't dangerous, in the sense that they don't install malware on your machine. In fact they're very handy for remembering your book preferences on Amazon.com. But cookies can be dangerous because they track your every move. Be particularly aware of this:

> When you log on to a website, you've given it permission to watch everything you do, everywhere you go, until you log back out! Even if you've left that site, if you didn't log out, it's still watching everything you do. Some, for instance that famous social network, track you even after you log out.

When you are done with a web site, to protect your privacy, *log out*. Ensure your browser is set to clear cookies, cache, temp files and history, then close the browser (not just the tab). Depending on the website and why you are there, you may wish to provide false information to avoid tracking. And you should be aware: some cookies (like Flash cookies) can survive "clearing" and can still be used to track you.

Confidentiality sounds very similar to privacy, but it's a different thing. If I don't know you have a crush on Betty or Bret, you've kept your privacy. If I know you're meeting behind the gym, your meeting is no longer private, but if I'm not watching it may still be confidential.

On the web, this means I may know you're visiting a site, but I can't read your communications because they're **encrypted** – scrambled so thoroughly you'd need a supercomputer and millions of years to decrypt them. When you visit a secure (HTTPS) web site, that's exactly what's it's doing. And it's using its certificate yet again to provide the **key** for that encryption. Is HTTPS totally safe? No, but it's the best we've got for now.

Exercises

4.48 Take a look at Google's **privacy policy**. Can you find it? Can you understand it? Compare it to the privacy policy of a retailer like Amazon.com. What about the privacy policy at social networking sites (SNS), such as Facebook?

4.49 Under these privacy policies, who can access your information? What can you do if the site violates its own policy? Can you take your information away?

Knowing If You Are Communicating Securely

If you have a private conversation, somebody could still find out about it. And even if it's confidential, somebody could be looking over your shoulder. (Search for "spy camera" to see why this is important.) So how can you be sure your communication is secure?

On the web, there are two major signals almost all browsers will give you that you are on a secure connection (using **HTTPS**, in other words). The first is the web protocol you see (or type) up in your URL address bar. If it's HTTP (which will look like **http://**), it is not secure, repeat, not secure.

You only have a secure connection when the protocol is HTTPS (so that the address starts with **https://**). While it's not visible, HTTPS is doing encryption, and unlike HTTP's port 80, HTTPS uses port 443.

The other visible cue in some browsers is a small **padlock icon** in the URL bar (or sometimes in the lower right corner of the window). If the lock is open or missing the connection is insecure, and if it's closed the connection is secure. Hover your mouse pointer over the lock, and in most cases a small message will appear telling you how long an encryption key is being used. Forty bits is very flimsy, while 128 bits is fairly stout, and the current standard.

Some newer browsers are using a feature like a "site button" - an area you can click near the URL address bar – which gives you security information about the site, though you may have to dig down to find the key length.

This is a good place to point out that while we use the term "secure connection" in this section, there is ultimately no such thing. The SSL/TLS encryption used by HTTPS is flawed and definitely can be cracked, if someone wants to crack it badly enough. You can probably trust it with Amazon.com (for now), but you should not trust it with your life. Why do we put it that way? Because in some countries, people literally do risk their lives accessing the web, and they should do it through a more secure technology called a **Virtual Private Network (VPN)**.

Methods of Verification

By now you've learned the basics of web security and privacy, and we hope you've thought about the things you could do as a hacker, or as the operator of a web site or server. Every decision you make will affect the security and privacy of real people – including you.

So how do you know if a server is secure, or a network, or an application? Should you trust the developers of the app or the OS? Will you be secure if you just keep your system updated?

The answers are, in order: Testing, No and No. We'll come back to testing, but when it comes to either applications or operating systems, manufacturers have proven over and over that you shouldn't necessarily trust them to get security right. (Read an **End User License Agreement** the next time you install software; you'll see that the manufacturer isn't responsible for anything at all!) And there are famous stories of updates that broke more things than they fixed, or introduced new vulnerabilities. Not to mention the **backdoors** that were discovered in some applications and operating systems!

When it comes to testing, the very best thing you can do is to think like a hacker. That's what this course is about. In other words, take advantage of other people's work. There are several security testing methodologies available, the results of contributions from hundreds of professionals. Just remember that any computer, network or application will change frequently, so test early and test often.

Methods arise from different philosophies. The **IT Infrastructure Library (ITIL)** is all about system life cycles; the **ISO 9000** standard deals with quality management systems. **ISECOM**, the organization that brings you Hacker Highschool, also provides a security testing methodology built on an opensource contributor model using open-source tools: the OSSTMM.

OSSTMM

The **Open Source Security Testing Methodology Manual (OSSTMM)** documents a widely-used and straightforward format for conducting security verifications. The individual tests in the OSSTMM aren't revolutionary, but the methodology itself allows anyone to conduct ordered tests with consistent professional quality.

The OSSTMM tests are divided into five sections:

- **Human Security**
- **Physical Security**
- **Wireless Security**
- **Telecommunications Security**
- **Data Networks Security**

You don't have to do every type of test; part of the methodology is doing only the relevant ones. This is where you can learn to be an expert: knowing which test to do, why to do it and when to do it.

To put it another way, the OSSTMM details the technical scope, but doesn't prescribe specific testing software. Instead, it describes:

- what should be tested

- the form in which the test results must be presented

- the rules for testers to follow to assure best results

- the **Attack Surface Metrics**, which put hard numbers on how much security you have

The OSSTMM is a document for professionals, but it's never too early to take a look at it and learn how it works. The concepts are thoroughly explained and are written in an easy-to-comprehend style.

Exercises

4.50 Patching is a necessary evil, and web administrators need to constantly patch code as new vulnerabilities are discovered. Search for a case in which a new problem arose from installing a security patch. Imaging you're a system administrator: would you argue for, or against, patching your systems immediately when the patches are released?

4.51 You've discovered that a patch will introduce a new vulnerability. Should the patch still be installed? Would it matter whether you have the source code or not?

4.52 Go to **http://cve.mitre.org** and find the button or link to search CVEs. When you find the right page, do a keyword search on "Apache". How many vulnerabilities are listed? (And consider: how many patches do you want to install? Is patching a realistic solution, or is it a cat and mouse game?)

4.53 Download a copy of the OSSTMM and review the methodology concepts. What principles can you learn from this methodology? Could you do a security audit based on the OSSTMM?

Feed Your Head: Understanding HTTP

Now that you have an understanding of how information flows, did you ever wonder how your web browser really asks for whatever it is you want to see online, and presents it to you?

What do you think the browsers ask for? What kind of information? We know that, depending on the website, we might have a few images, some animations, perhaps video. We also have text, and polls of different types. That is quite a lot of different things a web server has to send us, for us to properly enjoy a well formatted page, don't you think?

So, now you'll see EXACTLY what it is that your browser does, behind your back, so you can have a pleasant experience.

To help us in that task, we are going to install a Firefox extension called **httpfox**.

Httpfox monitors and analyzes all incoming and outgoing HTTP traffic between the browser and the webservers, so you get to see each individual request that is made.

Restart your Firefox browser, and now on the bottom right side you get an extra icon that you should click in order to open httpfox.

Press the icon, and then open a new tab and visit a couple of different websites. You now have a list of all the requests that your browser made.

Clear all of it, close all open Firefox tabs, start httpfox again and open www.isecom.org. Hit stop, and let's go through the requests.

The first thing that gets sent out of your browser, happens once you hit the enter key after typing www.isecom.org, and that's exactly what we see in httpfox.

Your browser does a GET request (as you can see from the Request Header), in HTTP 1.1. We are also saying that we want a specific host in that address, host www.isecom.org.

Consider the situation of a shared service provider. On one IP address, you could have hundreds of websites. This is possible exactly because of thie "host www.isecom.org" part of the request. If this functionality wasn't present, we could only have one domain per IP address, because the browser would have no way of telling what it really wants.

Now, because not all browsers are created equal, our browser is going to introduce himself, so the server can be sure to reply with information that suits us.

Next, we are telling the web server the kind of content that we are willing to accept. In this case, our browser says it accepts code written in HTML, XHTML and XML and would like to receive the information in American English (en-us) and what kind of encoding. If you have been to the ISECOM website before doing this capture, you will also see that we sent information regarding a cookie. A cookie is a small piece of data kept in your browser that stores information about a particular website. Almost every website you visit uses cookies. This information is used to serve you better (when it's not being used by the dark side of the force) because once you visit a website, you can be authenticated and so the website owner can greet you by your name, and present you with his content the way YOU want to see it. Think about the personalization that you can have on your online email application, for instance. All of this is for the GET request you instructed your browser to perform.

Now we will run through just three more lines. If you go to the "Content" tab, you will see the exact HTML code that was downloaded from the web server as a response to our previous GET request.

After the META tags, we got the following lines of code (at the time of writing):

```
<link rel="stylesheet" href="style.css" type="text/css" media="screen" />
<!--[if IE 6]><link rel="stylesheet" href="style.ie6.css" type="text/css"
media="screen" /><![endif]-->
<!--[if IE 7]><link rel="stylesheet" href="style.ie7.css" type="text/css"
media="screen" /><![endif]-->

<script type="text/Javascript" src="jquery.js"></script>
<script type="text/Javascript" src="script.js"></script>
```

Look at the highlighted pieces of code. You will find that the next three requests our browser made were exactly to those files. Notice that if we had Internet Explorer 6 for instance, we would have downloaded style.i6.css instead of downloading style.css. Different browsers, different code.

The rest of the files downloaded are more of the same. The browser interprets the HTML code it receives and makes decisions based on what it receives on the contents it should request next, depending on your behavior (clicking, mousing over, etc.).

Think about what all this means from a hacker's perspective. Everything your browser shows you are interpretations of what it receives from the servers. So could we somehow intercept this traffic and change how a client interacts with a server and vice versa? Of course it does... in another lesson.

Exercise

4.54 Aren't you curious what those .css, .js, and .swf files are? Try searching for those file extensions to learn a bit more about them. Explain them.

Going Deeper

While web hacking can go so much further because it's a huge, immense, monstrous field, you can't. You've reached the end of the line of what we can show you in this lesson. However, if web hacking is your thing, then here's a taste of the professional side of it all.

Passive Profiling and Intelligence Scouting

Quite frequently, employees within organizations leak pieces of seemingly innocent information to the Internet, and sometimes for quite valid reasons. However, when each of these pieces is brought together, a puzzle can be created forming a clearer picture of the internal workings of your organization than you would like. Hackers who know where to find these pieces of information may be able to generate a more directed attack against the organization, and each piece of information gleaned makes the attack just that much stronger.

So what types of information is a hacker searching for? Anything and everything that will help put the pieces of your organization's puzzle together including enumerating information relating to your organization, personnel and systems.

Organization Enumeration

Organization Enumeration concentrates on searching for business related information, such as the organizational hierarchy, departments, direction and planning, products and services, policies and processes, physical addresses, culture, regions, time zones, languages, alliances and partners, resellers, influential customers, vendors and distributors, investors, stocks and trading information, financial reporting, mergers and acquisitions, and anything else stated as confidential.

This allows a hacker to gain an understanding of the target organization, including possibly high level weaknesses providing the hacker with a strong knowledge base to launch an attack from. These weaknesses may be due to the ability to exploit trust relationships between various external parties, or where policies and processes are leaked to the public allowing an attacker to determine how to interact with the organization and the jargon required to do so.

Apart from gathering this information via Internet search engines, Corporate Information websites such as www.corporateinformation.com, biz.yahoo.com, and www.hoovers.com provide the public with detailed company information such as business summaries, financial blogs, analyst estimates and stock market statistics, insider information, executives names and pay details, news headlines and reports. Websites such as www.internalmemos.com allow hackers to search for internal memos, leaked emails, and rumors about specific organizations. This provides hackers with a clear insight into the business side of the organization, which may lead onto social engineering attacks being performed with much greater precision.

Personnel Enumeration

Personnel Enumeration entails seeking out employee names, email addresses, telephone and FAX numbers, office locations, training and skill requirements, job titles, job descriptions, employment histories, trust relationships between employees, pay scales, internal social politics, personnel dissatisfaction, turn-over rates, hirings and firings, social activities, hobbies, and personalities.

This type of information is generally seen by employees as insignificant, and is therefore leaked out onto the Internet with little or no thought or understanding of the impact that it may have on the security of the organization. By gathering personnel information, a hacker is able to passively develop a profile of various individuals and roles, allowing vulnerable employees to be enumerated and trusted users to be determined. One specific type of personnel that hackers attempt to profile is technical employees. Interactions with technical employees should be treated with caution as they are generally more security aware; however, they are highly sought after by hackers due to the likelihood that they have elevated privileges on the internal systems. Less technical staff members, as well as new staff members, are also popular targets as they aren't as likely to understand the implications of breaching the IT security policy, if they even know what the IT security policy consists of, and therefore may leak sensitive information to the Internet.

Personal Networking websites allow users to develop their professional and social networks; however, by registering with the website, a large portion of this information, including your list of contacts, is able to be searched and allows hackers to determine possible trust relationships that exist between people, or even allow the hacker to develop their own relationship with you. This may allow a hacker to exploit a trust relationship in order to get the user to perform an insecure action, such as revealing their username and password for a web application. Some Internet search engines also provide a "People Search" option, such as http://www.zoominfo.com, where profiles of people can almost instantly be created, revealing a large amount of public information found about an individual.

System Enumeration

System Enumeration aims at unveiling as much low-level technical information as possible, such as network registration, domain name registration, IP addresses and system names, corporate websites, virtual hosts, DNS entries, system configurations, administrative issues, types of servers and software used, physical server locations, production and development systems, possible usernames and passwords, and trust relationships between systems.

....

It amazes many people as to how much of this type of information is available on the Internet, and all you need to know is where to look or how to use an Internet search engine. Network registration information can be found via a number of public Whois databases, such as RIPE, ARIN, and APNIC. These databases allow users to determine what IP addresses your organization has been allocated, contact information revealing names, email addresses, phone numbers, physical addresses for the organization, and sometimes even the corporate DNS servers.

An attacker can then use this information to further their knowledge about the organization's systems by performing reverse lookups on the enumerated IP addresses. This allows hackers to determine names of systems, websites, domain names, and sub-domain names, which lead onto virtual hosts and email addresses being discovered.

Email addresses are specifically useful to hackers as they provide a point of contact for social engineering, they reveal the email address format of the organization allowing additional email addresses to be predicted, they allow Phishing attacks to be carried out, and can possibly be used to derive usernames for internal and external systems.

Internal system and software types and versions, as well as detailed system configurations are often found by looking at websites such as forums, blogs, newsgroups, mailing lists, web logs, intrusion logs and job databases. This is generally caused by employees carelessly posting internal system information to these websites from their corporate email addresses in an attempt to get assistance in troubleshooting that new internal server that just isn't working properly.

So before a hacker has even connected to your network they are likely to have built up a profile of your organization, your personnel, and your internal systems, allowing them to develop a much more directed and precise attack. This attack may be in the form of social engineering, exploiting a misconfigured web server, or by simply logging into external services with gathered authentication credentials.

Active Web Service Enumeration

To extend or verify the information gleaned during the passive profiling stage, an attacker may then move onto performing active web service enumeration. This entails actually connecting to the organization's systems to gather information that is generally not available through Internet search engines. This allows an attacker to see exactly what attacks are available to be carried out against the organization's employees and systems.

Port and Service Scans

If the hacker's aim was to be covert about their attack then they may choose to put off any port scanning and start with actively enumerating information from the organization's web services that were gathered during the passive profiling stage. If port scanning is not carried out with caution, Intrusion Detection Systems (IDSs) or Intrusion Prevention Systems (IPSs) may be triggered leading to administrators of the organization being alerted to the attack.

Additional web services may be uncovered by performing port scans against common web ports over TCP, such as 80, 81, 82, 83, 88, 90, 443, 880, 888, 1433, 4443, 8080, 8880, and 8888. The following code listing shows how nmap can be used to perform a simple scan for a subset of common web ports for a range of IP addresses. The "-P0" option skips the host discovery process and performs the scans even if the host does not appear to be up.

```
nmap -P0 -p80,443,8080 192.168.1.11-20
```

More advanced techniques can also be used to bypass firewalls or avoid detection by IDSs, such as fragmenting packets or setting the MTU, cloaking a scan with decoy probes, spoofing source IP addresses, setting the source port to 53, setting the TTL value, and sending packets with a bogus checksum.

Fingerprinting the Target

After the open web services have been discovered, the attacker now needs to fingerprint these services to determine what web servers and web server modules are running on the systems.

Fingerprinting can be performed in a variety of ways. Most port scanners can be configured to pull back banners or perform service and operating system predictions, giving the attacker an idea as to whether the open port is running a web service. Nmap uses the "-sV" and "-O" options to probe open ports to determine service and operating system version information, respectively. The "--version-intensity" option can also be used to set the probe intensity, with level 0 being light probing and level 9 sending every type of probe to the port.

```
nmap -P0 -sV -O --version-intensity 5 -p80,443,8080 192.168.1.11-20
```

This, however, does not allow the attacker to see all headers pulled back from the web server. The most verbose ways to see this information would be to connect to the web server port and issue an HTTP GET request manually, or by using a local web proxy, such as Paros or WebScarab. The code below demonstrates how an attacker using the netcat utility can connect to the web server and issue an HTTP GET request to retrieve the HTTP headers.

If the web service was running over HTTPS then the attacker could utilize the following stunnel command on Debian to create an encrypted SSL tunnel to the web service, and then use netcat again to issue the HTTP request.

```
stunnel -r https.example.com:443 -c -d localhost:888
nc localhost 888
GET / HTTP/1.0
```

A local web proxy could have also been used that would create the SSL tunnel automatically.

The HTTP Server header reveals information such as that the system is a UNIX server, what version of Apache is running, and which modules are installed to enhance the web server's functionality, as well as other information such as the server date. An attacker can then use this information to determine whether any vulnerabilities and exploits exist for these specific software versions by looking at various public vulnerability and exploit databases (just search for them since they seem to move a lot). If the attacker is skilled and determined enough then they could also download this specific version of Apache and develop their own exploits for the system in an attempt to gain a remote shell on the host.

Hacking
Passwords

Introduction to Hacking Passwords

To enter your home, you need a key for the locked door (unless you can pass through walls, which would be really cool). If you have a locker at school or in gym class, you either have a key lock or have a number combination lock to get inside the locker. If you want books from your library, you have to have a library card to prove who you are. You need drivers licenses, school IDs, and lunch passes to prove you are who you say you are and that you've got a lunch coming.

There are hundreds of ways we protect our stuff, using locks or guards, fences and gates to elaborate video surveillance cameras. Security professionals focus on physical security and digital security to maintain confidentiality, control access, to authenticate users, and to enforce non repudiation. The really good security professionals use combat attacks dogs trained in at least ten forms of martial arts along with special training from the FBI, the CIA, MI5, and the KGB. These dogs are super vicious and will rip out your jugular if you don't rub their bellies first. If you have a dog treat, they'll play fetch for hours on end.

In this lesson, we're going to take a hard look at how passwords work, what they can do, and what they can't do. Like any other tool, passwords have many uses but also have flaws if they are not used properly. Each day, passwords to accounts are compromised or stolen or just guessed by someone who shouldn't have access to that account. Having a weak password is much like leaving your house unlocked with all the windows left wide open.

Over the past forty years, countless studies have been conducted on passwords. Believe it or not users create and never change really crappy passwords all the time. Study after study shows how 99.9% of all Internet users have weak (easily cracked) passwords and use these lousy passwords for multiple accounts. Worse yet, we also choose bad login names. So, most of the users on the Internet have easy to guess passwords and we use the same login names. Isn't that convenient?

Hacking is easier and easier since more people add themselves to the Internet each day. What are worse (and things do get worse) are is that names and passwords are the primary access control used by most websites. A long running survey by Microsoft shows that most common passwords are six to eight digits long, and user names are on average only six digits long.

Before we start hunting for passwords, we need to know quite a bit more about how passwords work. We also need to learn how to crack passwords and how to create strong passwords. This lesson can get kind of dangerous because cryptology is involved here. If you don't do well with math or if complex algorithms make you nauseous, read slowly and breathe deep. Grab a paper bag in case you hyperventilate.

We are going to get into the weeds on passwords, digging deep down where the really fun stuff lives. Hold onto your seat belt because it's going to be a wild ride.

Pins, Passwords and Personal Poop

You are unique, just like everyone else in the world. You look different, smell different, think different, walk and talk different than every person you've ever or will ever meet. Sometimes you smell so different that others don't want to be around you. It is easy for you to see your own uniqueness and for you to recognize the differences in those around you. Once in a while you might confuse someone with somebody else but overall we humans are excellent at recognizing faces in a crowd. The problem is how do you prove you are who you say you are to a stranger? Even worse, how do you prove you are you to a computer?

Computers are not that good at being able to spot a single person out of a crowd like we are. Programs are getting better but they are no match for our matching abilities. When you meet somebody for the first time we usually introduce ourselves by our name, followed by some greeting or body contact like a hand shake, hug, kiss on the cheek or punch in the nose (depending on the situation). This introduction is based on your own culture and how those around you greet each other. Some cultures bow at the waist, others hug and kiss one another, while even more just nod and smile. This is how we introduce ourselves and start our first impression.

Deep inside our minds we are sampling their smell, the color of their eyes, the hair style they have, what sort of clothes they are wearing and a million other subconscious sensory inputs are taking place. Based on previous personal experience, we catalog each new contact and form an opinion about whether we like or don't like that person. This forms a trust bond in our emotions as to whether we are pleased to see this person or we really aren't sure about them. Computers don't have this ability, which is good for some of us.

Systems need a way to determine if the user is who they say they are. We call this **authentication** which is part of **access control**. Yeah, this is where passwords come in. We need to verify your identification for you to access this device. Usually this is done in combination with a user name. Using just a password and a user name is single factor authentication. In the spectrum of security, we are looking for something that only you know, something you are and something you have. A password is something you know and your user name is something you are. If a token, a fob, credentials, digital certificates or an ID card is also required, than that is something you have. The same holds true for using your smartphone to verify a text with a code because your phone is something you have. Plus that provides two-factor authentication.

Biometrics approaches this by using your physical features to prove your identification through eye blood vessel patterns, finger prints, voice input, breath, facial features, earlobes, microbes on your body, and other aspects of your body that are unique to you. Passwords are a cheap and easy method to partially prove you are who you say you are. These are the basic flaws with passwords: they are easy to forget, easy to lose, easy to steal, easy to replace, hard to remember and too easily direct blame at the person who has their account hacked. Then again, if your biometric password is stolen, you can't just change your fingers.

Feed Your Head: CAPTCHA and Passwords

CAPTCHA has single-handedly kept more morons from posting stupid opinions on blogs and websites than any other technology ever and thereby keeps the Internet from crumbling under the full weight of the stupid part of humanity.

You know CAPTCHA. It's that box with hard-to-read words that you need to type in before posting to websites. It's interesting because it adds a new channel to authentication, the human channel, and it adds entropy for slowing down the attack by making a complicated extra step in the process. It's meant to prevent SPAMMERS and password cracking attacks. If a password is a key then CAPTCHA is a special twist of the key if I may. That's good. Too bad most people find reading mutilated letters off a paisley background more than enough entropy to slow them to a stop.

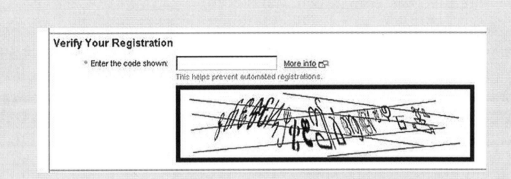

CAPTCHA is impossible for some and frustrating for the rest of the people. Too bad computers didn't have the same trouble. If we are at risk of the Matrix or Skynet it will be because of CAPTCHA. It's so annoying that if the Terminators wanted to end humanity they would put CAPTCHA on our Internet-connected refrigerators and watch us starve to death.

Methods of Authentication: Passwords

The first step in obtaining proper access to any important information or secure area is to prove you should have access to it. In order to gain that access, we need to authenticate ourselves to the system. Authenticating is just fancy word for proving you are who you say you are. You know who you are but strangers and networks need some proof that you're not pretending to be somebody else. Depending on the sensitivity of access, security folks look for at two or three items. This is known as **multi-factor authentication.** We are looking for **something you know, something you have** and **something you are.**

Something you know is just a piece of information that only you should know. For example, only you and a few select other people would know your favorite color, favorite food, all-time greatest movie, or your password. This information could include the school you last attended, the name of your pet, the sport and position you like to play, favorite music or book and so forth.

Something you have might be the token you were given for access to a network. It could be your key to the lock or even an identification card. This is usually something that you would physically have in your procession. You must have that on you to gain access to that network as part of multi-factor authentication.

Something you are is unique only to you. This is a big topic for biometrics because it can involve your fingerprint, which have been proven to not be unique and easily spoofed. However, there are other things about you that are much more provable such as the blood vessels in your iris, the speed at which you type on a keyboard, your thought patterns, your behavior and all kinds of other aspects that make you who you are.

Passwords come into play as something you know. The logic behind using passwords is that only an authorized agent would know the correct password to gain access. (See any problems there?)

There are three main types of passwords.

Feed Your Head: Multifactor Authentication

Multi-factor Authentication is like having two passwords or a way to confirm a password that comes from somewhere else. A common way is with a login on a website that requires an extra code that you enter in addition to your password. That code is changed every minute and it could come to you by SMS or it could be on a calculator-looking token you carry with you. There's many more types though.

The concept of multi-factor authentication being more secure comes from it being harder. It's mathematically harder to guess and it's physically harder to copy.

And because it's harder it takes more time which introduces more entropy into the authentication process. That means attackers have fewer guesses possible in a given time, generally time enough for security to be alerted and respond.

But is harder more secure, or does harder just limit the number of people willing to try to break it? Harder actually makes the pool of capable criminals shallow and small. At least until one of them makes a tool that makes it easier for other criminals and starts growing the pool.

So is harder more secure or does it lower risk? What's the difference? Does it matter? I'm glad you asked.

Look at a bank ATM PIN entry. It adds entropy as touch keys and annoying menu delays to slow you and an attacker down to prevent brute forcing of the 10,000 possible combinations of a 4 digit PIN before a bank worker notices.

But it's really a type of additional password that slows down humans who can't type a PIN faster. It's an additional password that you can't know as long as you're human because you'll always be too slow to know it.

See that? Problem – humans guessing many combinations. Solution – make it harder for them to try. Result – we narrowed the pool of potential criminals to only those who can afford a Raspberry Pi to make a robot hand to guess many combinations.

So making it harder for a criminal to attack only works as long as criminals can't find a way to make it easier. So is it secure? Here's a simpler example:

The second story window on a house is open. The thief would need a ladder or some climbing skills to get in. Is that house secure against thieves? No. It's less risky than leaving the first floor window open but as long as any window is open that only makes it harder to break in. Until it's made easier by some tool or skill.

So lets look at this multi-factor authentication again. It's authentication at least 2 different ways. It could be a password and an SMS retrieved code. It could be a password and an added number from a token. It could be a login and a threatening phone call to the helpdesk with a lot of attitude.

Technically, and we're not claiming this is right, but even CAPTCHA before a login/password could pass for 2-factor authentication under this shady definition (maybe ATM PIN number pads need to add a CAPTCHA to also make it harder for the thieving robots).

Then you see if we make it harder to break or steal something, it's not the same as making it secure. And therefore two-factor authentication isn't actually more secure, it's just special because it makes breaking a password harder. It's like it's the password that gets to stay on the bouncy castle because its parents own it.

But remember how we also said ideally in a perfect world people shouldn't be making their own passwords or protecting them either? Unfortunately, this broken thing called multi-factor authentication is the best answer we've got now to make it better.

Strings of Characters: Something You Know

At the most basic level, authentication uses passwords, which are words or strings of characters (numbers and symbols). A keyboard or keypad allows entry of these types of passwords. These passwords range from the simplest – such as the three digit codes used on some garage door openers – to the more complicated combinations of characters, numbers and symbols that are recommended for protecting highly confidential information.

The problem with character based passwords is that the more complicated the password is, the harder it is to remember. The classic solution is writing the password down on a slip of paper next to the computer screen. If you're going to write down a password, keep the paper in your wallet or purse! People rarely lose their wallet or purse and if they do, changing your passwords will be a snap compared to replacing all their credit cards and their drivers license.

Strings of Characters Plus a Token: Something You Know plus Something You Have

The next level in authentication (**two-factor authentication**) is to require a password plus a **token** of some type. An example of this is the ATM, which requires a card – the token – plus a personal identification number or PIN. This is considerably more secure, because if you lack either item, you are denied access.

There are all kinds of token based systems out there. One of the current attack trends is for attackers to attach a card scanner (a **skimmer**) in front of an ATM machine's card reader. When a victim inserts their card into the ATM, they enter their PIN. The skimmer reads the magnetic strip off the victim's card and also captures the PIN. The victim is completely unaware of this crime until their bank account is emptied.

The point here is that tokens can be hacked and have been hacked.

Biometric Passwords: Something You Are

The third level in authentication is biometrics. This is the use of non-reproducible biological features, such as fingerprints or facial features, to control access. An example of this is the retinal scan, in which the retina – which is the interior surface of the back of the eye – is photographed. The retina contains a unique pattern of blood vessels that are easily seen and this pattern is compared to a reference. Biometric authentication is the most sophisticated and is considered safer, but it has failed. How about copying someone's fingerprint with a gummy bear, and then using it to authenticate as another person? (Been done.) And hey, if they just need your retina, that's not so tricky, is it?

A reality TV show demonstrated the use of clear plastic tape to copy a fingerprint and fool a fingerprint scanner. Lately, the whole idea that fingerprints were unique to every individual has come under fire. There have been several recent criminal cases where one person's fingerprint matched another person. Like most science based on human characteristics, there's still plenty of work to be done before biometrics can be considered fool-proof.

Let's also keep in mind that science can only prove that something is wrong, it can never prove that something is right. All theories are just theories until they are proven wrong. That is the job of science.

Exercises

4.1 Is the SIM card in your cellphone an authentication token or a tracking device? Pull the SIM card out of your phone and see if you can still connect to another cellphone.

4.2 Going CSI, try to capture your own or a friend's fingerprint using clear tape. What additional materials do you need to get a "good" print?

4.3 Now, try to capture a friend's print without their knowledge. Hint: glass works nicely, even though TV investigators get prints off of everything imaginable, even water.

4.4 Switch your cellphone SIM card with another cellphone and try to make a phone call. Now go back to the first exercise question and rethink your original answer. If you got the answer right the first time, take a break and grab a glass of water.

Game On: Hungry for Knowledge

Mokoa's stomach groaned next to the gold-fish tank. Several small orange swimmers looked at the teen with worry, hoping he wasn't in the mood for seafood. Gerbils across the aisle hid their apple and vegetable bits behind their water bottle. Even though the pet store was filled with food, none of it was human food.

Mokoa complained to himself that he shouldn't have eaten his lunch so early. It was late afternoon and he was running the store by himself. He also forgot to get a snack from his upstairs room before he started his shift. Normally this wouldn't be a problem because he could just run upstairs and grab a quick bite. However, every time he started up the stairs, another customer would enter the store. Every time.

It was one of those days where a certain customer would come into the store and just ask questions or want to see one thing after another, never buying anything. Mokoa had to treat them with respect and reply to every question or request, because he was the pet store owners grandson. And he was on shift.

But he was also very hungry.

The demanding customer asked to see the bottom bag in a pile of 50 lb. bags of dry dog food. The stack was ten bags tall. The teen pet seller smiled outwardly but truly wanted to throw a bag of food on top of the annoying customer. Using two ladders, Mokoa had just moved the eighth dog food bag when the customer changed his mind. He didn't want the last bag anymore. He now wanted the 50 lb. bag that was on the bottom of the new pile now.

As he stood next to the ladder trying to figure out if he could throw a 50 lb. bag on the customer and tell the police a convincing story, Jace stepped through the front door.

Trumpets blew. Heavenly lights flared behind her. Angels sung in chorus. Jace was here.

"Jace, you are the best thing I've seen all day," Mokoa announced throughout the store.

She squinted her light sensitive eyes, unsure if Mokoa was joking or had some sort of illness. Jace approached him to check his forehead temperature.

Mokoa looked at his best friend and said, "I'll be right back. Hold down the store for me, will ya."

He was upstairs in a single step.

Jace turned to the customer and asked, "What is this all about?"

By the time Mokoa returned to the downstairs store, his milk mustache was almost gone. He almost forgot about Jace, now that his tummy was close to being full. Mokoa held a plate with three cookies on it. As he looked around the store, he didn't see Jace but he did notice that the piles of dog food were neatly stacked in their original location. The nagging customer was gone so the teen grabbed a chair and started to sit behind the cash register desk.

"Hey, ouch! Move that thing. I was here first," Jace yelped.

Mokoa saw Jace laying on the floor using her knapsack as a pillow.

"What are you doing down there," he asked as he set the plate on the chair.

"Resting, where you been?"

"I needed some food. When you came in, I finally had a chance to grab a bite. Thanks for covering for me," Mokoa said. "Where did that customer go? Did he buy anything?"

Jace gathered herself up and said,"Naw, he was just looking. I got him to put those bags away before he left, though. Hey, thanks for bringing me some cookies for my effort."

"Hands off. They're mine. Don't touch or else," he said in a defensive posture.

"Or else what," Jace replied.

"Or else I'll do something," Mokoa said.

Jace mocked, "You'll do something, I'll bet."

Mokoa guarded the cookie plate and said, "I will and I'll take that bet."

"What bet," Jace knew Mokoa was losing this argument. Now was a good time to show him who is the brains in this team. "Tell you what, I'll bet you those three cookies that I can guess your laptop password in under 90 seconds," she said.

Mokoa replied, "And what if you don't guess it in 90 seconds. What do I get out of the bet?"

Jace thought about for a second before she replied, "Then, I'll teach you how to crack passwords. Deal?"

"Deal," he replied. He always wanted to learn some of her skills but she never taught him anything.

Mokoa grabbed his laptop and handed it over to Jace. She smiled back.

The teen hacker inspected the outside of the machine and began her lecture, "First off, guessing passwords isn't terribly difficult. The more you know about the victim, the better guesses you can make to unlock that password. For example, knowing your name is a step towards knowing your username. Many times, usernames and passwords are the same or very similar. People are lazy; they don't want to remember too many things."

"With something portable like a laptop, a keyboard, or a phone, the password is sometimes written on the outside of the device. Users love to keep passwords on post-its under their keyboard or next to their computer screen. It looks like you didn't write your password on the outside of your computer so you did good there," Jace said as she spied Mokoa for a reaction.

With the laptop turn on and ready for the password, Jace studied the screen. "I will need to know how many attempts I can try and guess your password before it locks me out. Most people disable this security feature and allow anyone to guess their password forever. I suggest you set password attempts to between five and ten attempts. In fact I remember telling you this when you bought this computer last year. Let's see if you listened to my advice," Jace said as she tried a few basic passwords.

"Nope, you didn't set a password limit," she said with an evil laugh. Jace cracked her knuckles and started to whistle the tune from Clint Eastwood's movie The Good, the Bad, and the Ugly.

Game continues...

Password Biology: SWAT

Passwords rule most of the digital world. In particular, passwords rule the entire Internet world. (When was the last time a website asked for your fingerprint?) To take a closer look at passwords we need a tool to open them up. The toolset we'll be using today is called SWAT. **SWAT** stands for Strengths, Weaknesses, Advantages, and Threats. Put on your lab coats and slap on those protective goggles because it's going to get messy.

Strengths

Size matters when it comes to passwords. The longer the password, the more difficult it becomes to crack. At a certain length, a password becomes essentially too expensive to crack. Hackers are busy people, very busy. They want to direct their computing power toward easy passwords. If you have a password that is six digits long, an attacker will focus on you instead of someone whose password is twelve digits long. Cracking a password requires time and resources. For each additional character added to a password, complexity increases exponentially.

The word **entropy** describes the difficulty of cracking any password using brute force, pure guessing, using a collection of common passwords or just relying on dictionaries. This is why many systems limit the number of times you can enter an incorrect password before the system locks you out for a specific time. When it comes to passwords (because the term is also used in physics), entropy is usually measured in bits: the number of bits required to make up a password. For instance, an 8-character password requires 8 bits per character (in English, but not in all languages – some need 16 bits per character) so 8x8=64, meaning an 8-character password space has 64 bits of entropy. And to put it simply, the more entropy, the stronger the password.

Another major strength for using passwords is they are customizable for each user. Passwords are not stored, only the password hash is stored. If you haven't met MD5 yet, we'll get into the hash stuff a little later. Just be sure to know that any change to a password, such as capitalizing a letter in it, will produce a completely different hash output.

Feed Your Head: Understanding Password Hashes

Passwords can be stored in plain text format ("password") or as a hashed value (MD5 hash of the word password: 5f4dcc3b5aa765d61d8327deb882cf99).

The hashed value of a password string is generated by a mathematical process or algorithm that produces a different string depending on the algorithm used: MD5, SHA3 and so on; each uses different cryptographic operations.

Let's say you want to log in to a username/password protected website. First you'll have to set up your login details. You create a username and enter a password. What happens when you hit submit?

Most websites run your password through a cryptographic hash function like the one mentioned above and then store it in a database. Here is an example of how a PHP script would hash your password before it is stores it in a database.

```
$Password = MD5($_POST['password']);
```

In this line of PHP code, the script takes the password you submitted via $_POST and runs it through the MD5() cryptographic hash function, which transforms the submitted password into its MD5 hash value. Then the hash is stored in the variable $Password so it can be passed to the database.

Now that you have your login details created, next time you go to login, the PHP script will take the password you enter, run it through the hash function and compare it to the hash stored in the database. If the two hashes match, it means that the password submitted is the same password stored in the user database, so the website will log you in. Here's an example in pseudo-code.

```
If (md5($Submitted_Password) == $Stored_Password_Hash) Then
Login()
Display_Wrong_Login_Details_Message()
```

Exercises

4.5   In Linux, in a terminal, create a new file using the touch command:

```
touch testfile.txt
```

Now put some text in it by using the redirect character (>):

```
echo This is a test > testfile.txt
```

Now use the MD5sum command to generate the unique hash or digest value of that file:

```
md5sum testfile.txt
```

You will get a long hash value back. Look at it carefully, then add to the text in your test file using the append operator (>>):

```
echo . >> testfile.txt
```

Run the md5sum command again. Compare the new hash value to the one you got before.

4.6 In Windows, find, download and install **MD5deep**. Try it out with a test file you create in Wordpad or Notepad. Then make a change to the file and compare the hash values.

Weaknesses

Everything that was just covered as a strength is also a weakness. The size of a password adds additional security but it also adds complexity. Humans are lazy creatures; we want to make things as simple as possible for ourselves. From a security professional view, security should be invisible and effortless to the user. Security should not hamper or slow down work but should operate in the background. Anytime you add additional steps or requirements to the work environment, you slow down work performance. You might have noticed that security is not anywhere near that goal at this point.

As the need for stronger passwords are enforced by the boss, people will always find a way to get around such mandates. The average adult can memorize seven characters. Asking a user to memorize twelve characters means that the person will have to either create a password that ends with 12345 or one that they will write down. Worse yet, they will reuse passwords over and over again. Think of what will happen when a user is told they must have a password that is eighteen characters long! You don't really want to be on either side of that conversation.

On top of mandating a twelve or eighteen digit password, add in a requirement to change that password every ninety days (without repeating any of the characters from your previous ten passwords, welcome to the U.S. Department of Defense). You and you users are going to be overwhelmed with memorization. Go ahead, try to enforce this on your family.

Managing ten or twenty users accounts is fairly easy, but most big organizations have hundreds or thousands of users. Managing passwords and logins for larger groups becomes a full time job. Sooner or later it will be a highly hackable mess. From a password management standpoint, removing an account by deleting the user and their password is inexpensive and fairly easy to do. Any hacker knows that administrators often fail to do this, which makes for easy fishing.

Over the years several organizations have been caught storing passwords in clear text. One of the most recent examples was a major attack on Sony Entertainment in November 2014. Thousands of usernames and passwords were discovered and released to the public by attackers that showed Sony had stored this information in their networks as easy to read text. Your best bet is to not store passwords at all but rather store the hash values instead. Even then, the hash values need to be secure too.

Feed Your Head: Understanding the Keyspace

The **keyspace** is the set of all valid combinations of characters and letters. For instance, a keyspace that includes uppercase and lowercase letters (26 x 2) and numbers from 0 to 9 would contain 62 possible values for each position. To make things simple, consider the smaller keyspace of 26 letters and 10 digits. It's a common mistake to calculate the possibilities wrong. If you use a 2-character password, and there are 36 possible characters for each position, that's 2 to the 36th power, right?

No. A password of 2 characters from a character set of 26 letters and 10 digits is not 2^{36}, but 36^2. You have 36 choices for the first character and can combine them with 36 choices for the next character. 1296 different passwords are possible.

Similarly a password of 8 characters from a character set of 26 letters and 10 digits is not 8^{36}, but 36^8. So roughly 2,820,000,000,000 different passwords are possible.

It's also a mistake to say that passwords must contain certain sub-charactersets. This is easiest to see with a 2-character password from the above set, but with the requirement that it has to contain at least one digit and at least one letter. For letter + digit there are 26x10=260 different passwords possible and for digit + letter there are 10x26=260 different passwords possible, a total of 520 different passwords. That's less than half of the original 1296 different passwords. Because there are rules about the construction of the passwords, some combinations are invalid, and every invalid combination decreases the size of the keyspace, making it weaker.

Now we have to say that complexity rules are invented for a reason. That reason is laziness (or stupidity, or both). Many people choose weak passwords because they are easy to enter (123456, qwerty, qazwsx, 123qwe, 000000, etc.) or easy to remember (pet's names, kid's names, favorite brand, favorite sports team, dictionary words etc.).

To prevent such "weak" passwords someone had the bad idea to require complexity in the passwords. Others had an even worse idea to like this and spread the idea. You can read the explanation below and do the math yourselves to find out that such rules eliminates millions or billions of perfectly fine eight character passwords.

How many easy-to-enter or easy-to-remember bad passwords do you think exist? If you add all simple keyboard sequences, pet names, kid names etc. you can think of and the English, Dutch and Pakistan word lists together you likely won't even reach a million. So how about getting rid of complexity rules and allowing all combinations, except the ones on the blacklist? That blacklist doesn't have to contain a million existing words and names; it's effective when it contains just the top 1000 most used passwords in the leaked password lists that are widely available nowadays.

Even if you only put the top 100 most used passwords on the black list, the chances that someone brute-forces the right password is less than when you use biometrics. Remember the news that the iPhone5 fingerprint reader can be fooled by latex fingers (reproduced from fingerprints left on a cup)? Therefore today biometrics are only useful as a second factor in authentication. This might change some time in the future when accuracy has raised to a sufficient level or if you can get new fingerprints in case yours get compromised.

Realize that affordable biometric equipment had an error rate of worse than 1% in 2011. Now suppose that with current technology this has decreased to 0.1%. This still is pretty inaccurate. A single try on a three digit password gives you about the same chances of gaining access.

Strong passwords are long or complex (many types of characters). That's it. They have to require many guesses. This is the main thing. Further, to allow for more complexity, you should allow as many characters in the character set as possible with no restrictions. Any restriction reduces the keyspace.

There is an exception for Microsoft Windows with (ancient) NTLM compatibility, where passwords are stored as 2 hashes in 2 chunks of 7 bytes each. Using a password of 15 characters of more eliminates that risk, because NTLM can only handle passwords of up to 14 characters; anything longer and the NTLM version simply isn't saved. This is why a sharp hacker will look for those weak NTLM hashes, and why a sharp security engineer disables their use completely: modern Windows supports much longer passwords – and you should use them.

Advantages

How much does a password cost? Each password costs an organization a tiny bit of computation and storage (to hold it and look it up) but not much more than air costs you to breathe. Other forms of authentication can cost an organization a small fortune to install, maintain and operate. A lost password is easy to reset or replace. Passwords can be generated and distributed *en mass* in no time at all.

Users can be allowed to customize their own password as long as it meets expected security requirements. Passwords can't get lost like a physical token can. If a token goes missing, the token replacement requirements can be expensive and harmful to the longevity of the employee (you can get fired). Passwords can be replaced in a matter of seconds and a compromised password can be revoked easily.

If more than one person decides to share a password for easy access, that account can be audited and taken off-line. The password would be changed, as well as the login. Passwords can be traceable to the user if suspicious events need to be investigated.

Of course, this also means a criminal could hide her actions behind someone else's account. Isn't that handy? Unless you're the victim.

Threats

The last tool in our tool set is Threats. There are many areas of concern to acknowledge when it comes to password threats. The easiest of these threats to attempt would be password guessing. Thanks to the Internet, there are many resources available for guessing passwords. For example, fire up your search engine of choice and search for "common passwords." Start compiling the common passwords from your results into a single location and before you know it you'll have a great password dictionary to assist you with password guessing.

Social Engineering is another great way to determine a users password. You would be amazed at how many people use the names of their children, spouse's name, pet names, anniversary or birth dates, favorite color, etc. for their password or as a combination to make up their password. All of this information can be gathered from someone through casual conversation or examining the articles in their office or cube. The best way to prevent against this form of attack would be avoiding the use of any information that may be common knowledge.

Dumpster Diving and shoulder surfing can also provide quite a bit of useful information about someone that can be used to guess their password. Being aware of your surroundings, using a screen protector, not facing your monitor towards a window and using a cross-cut shredder can assist you in protecting against those threats.

With the large amount of social media platforms now available, it's getting even easier to find out information about people. You can probably get someone's favorite color, birthday, kids names and spouse's name right from their Facebook page. Be cautious of the information that you share via social media and keep strong privacy controls in order to help reduce the threat of attackers phishing for information that can be used to guess passwords.

Phishing may be the easiest and most popular way to get account details. In a phishing attack the cracker sends a link to a fake login page via email or chat. The unwitting victim clicks, sees a familiar login page and enters their credentials. Often from there they're redirected to the real login page, where they will be confusingly not logged in. Oh well, try it again. But by now the cracker has the victim's login details

Keyloggers, RATs and other malware can set up a keylogger or RAT server on the victim. Your boss can do it too, using either software or a slick little piece of hardware that plugs in between your keyboard and your computer. The keylogger records every key stroke of the victim. Everything you type, the keylogger records and sends to the cracker. Some malware will look for the existing web browser's client password list and copy it to a remote cracker, making the passwords easily accessible if they aren't encrypted.

Consider this: when you answer **password reset questions**, do you use the real answer? We know we don't and we recommend that you do not either. Password reset questions are a great way for attackers to guess your password. Next time you answer one of those questions, think of something other than the real answer to use. For example, come up with a strategy that says, each time you see the question, "What was the make of your first car?" you answer it with the word "Chocolates." We all know there are a limited number of car manufacturers, so it would be pretty easy for a person to rip through a list of car makers. We seriously doubt anybody would be guessing "Chocolates" for the make of your first car.

In order to help decrease the number of password threats you are exposing yourself to, get in the habit of following best practices such as memorizing passwords instead of writing them down, not reusing passwords and creating strong passwords. The creation of strong passwords will be discussed later in this lesson.

Another important threat is the password reuse. A long time ago in a galaxy far, far away an important website was compromised via SQL Injection and attacker found passwords stored with weak hash algorithms and e-mail addresses users used to register. The attacker tried – with a lot of success – e-mails and associated password on various social network and posted malicious messages containing a malware. This is an important lesson: never use the same passwords on different services, are you using same passwords? Change now! Have you difficulties to generate or remember complex passwords? Use hints in this lesson and a good password manager.

Segregation is your friend. On web sites, enable **HTTPS Only** in your browser to ensure that the site uses an encrypted connection whenever data is exchanged. Your browser will now keep you from going to an insecure website that might ask for data.

Take also care of sharing your password, also with friends. On some web sites terms of use – these are an **Indemnification control**, see the OSSTMM for details – you are responsible for all activities generated with your credential.

Human Biology

Memory

We store every bit of sensory information our body interacts with for a fraction of a second in the cranial cortex (your noggin). Some of that input is moved into our short-term memory, such as parts of a conversation with your parents or your math teacher showing you your grades. The sensory data that catches our attention, like the school bell ringing or your smelly socks under the bed, will stay in short-term memory throughout the cortex. This short bit of excitement stays in our memory for just a few seconds, perhaps a minute.

Studies from the Harvard School of Medicine indicate that the average adult can memorize nine random items, characters, numbers, or other unimportant items for up to a week. After that week, our capacity for memory drops down to seven items. If the collection of random items are not utilized, or rehearsed, these seven items slowly fade in less than three weeks.

If we do not attach some sort of meaning to random objects for later retrieval, those items will not be moved into our long-term memory. This plays an important role when working with lists, tasks, combinations, events, recollection, and passwords. If we can associate new information with old memories or past events, those new memories will become locked in long-term brain storage.

Basically, humans can't be expected to memorize long strings of characters and random digits if there's no real meaning behind them. This is one of major faults with computer generated passwords when you are strictly forbidden to write them down. (Welcome to black ops.) How can you be expected to remember a string of eight, ten, or twelve characters when your short-term memory is maxed out within one minute? Try telling this to your mom when you forgot her birthday, again.

The problem is most networks have a password update policy that is almost impossible to comply with. These policies require the user to have a password of nine characters or more but not more than twelve. The password must be a combination of upper and lower case words, have numbers and special characters. The system stores your previous ten passwords and you must pick a new password every 45 days. This is where a password manager comes in.

One of the problems with such a policy is that people can't remember such long passwords, nor do they have the creativity to make new ones and remember them every 45 days. Plus, passwords usually start off with a capital letter and end with number or special characters. That makes cracking this policy even easier.

Bad Habits

As our lives become more dependent on fast electronic devices and a speedier world, where we are expected to do more in less time, our attention span narrows. School teachers report that thirty years ago they could focus the entire class on a single subject for over an hour. Now, these same instructors are reporting that they have to change topics or refocus the students every eight minutes. Our attention span is shorter as we are getting accustomed to instantaneous stimulation ever minute of the day. The worse part of all this constant content, is that we think we can perform more activities at the same time, or multitask. College students and new workers who enter the world confidently proclaim their skills of conducting four and five tasks at the same time, with the same level of accuracy as focusing on a single task.

Research at the Massachusetts Institute of Technology (MIT) tells a completely different story. Three independent studies found that individuals who think they can perform many tasks at the same time, with a high level of accuracy, fail miserably when tested. The test subjects were carefully selected to ensure they had scored fairly high on academic tests and used smart-phones to tweet, socialize, research, email, answer calls and other activities we associate with the "tech generation."

Each test group was given one main task to perform such as writing a policy letter or typing a memo without errors. As the testing progressed, the test subjects began to receive messages, texts, requests for chat, emails that needed to be answered with researched information, and other multitasking activities at set intervals. The test subjects failed to perform a single task. Each task was full of simple errors and many tasks included answers that belonged to a different task.

The next phase of this study added one more critical element sponsored by the National Traffic Safety Council (NTSC), driving a simulated car. One in ten students were able to back out of a simulated driveway and move down the road one block before they crashed due to multitasking. Again, each task that was added to the main objective of driving a car was nothing more than answering a call, checking an email and looking up a traffic report on a smart-phone with a cup of water in the test subject's lap. Sound familiar? That's because millions of drivers are over confident in their ability to accomplish several tasks at one time. Our brains were not designed to handle the complexity brought on by modern technology. Instead of making life easier, it just makes our lives run at a faster pace.

We Want Change

We are creatures of habit. We want to conform to our environment just as we want to be accepted by our peers. We also need to make our lives comfortable but interesting. This combination causes mankind to resist change, more specifically, abrupt change.

In the world of security we preach to our users the basic principles of using long passwords, using upper and lower case, changing passwords, and not using the same password for all accounts. However loud and long security folks bang this message into everyone's head, it's still hard to change habits. Resistance to change is what makes hacking passwords so easy, unless some incentive to use strong passwords is applied (like keeping your job).

Incentives can be either positive or negative. A positive incentive would be something as simple as a little banner telling a user that their password is strong or a pat on the back by their supervisor. A negative incentive would be getting fired because their account was hacked due to a weak password. If you're a security professional, you will need to find a balance between the two forms of incentives. If you're hacking the system, you can use them to your advantage.

Humans respond better and longer to a positive incentive than a negative one. Think about it this way: do you like being yelled at for having a bad grade or would you rather be given a cash reward for earning good grades? Cash, right? In the security arena, humans have been and always will be the weak link for a security environment. You will need to "sell security" to your peers, your friends, and your family. You can start by looking at the current password policy your organization has and work up from there. What – you don't have one?

Feed Your Head: Bad Passwords Are Your Problem

Many places claim that a criminal hacker got into an account because the user made a bad password. That's just shifting blame. The truth is that the password problem isn't a people problem. It's an authentication problem.

The thing is that people are people. It's too easy (and cheap) to put the responsibility on just regular people for making uncrackable passwords despite security researchers (and anyone with common sense) knowing that really good passwords are too long and too hard to remember so they can't really exist in a realistic, usable state. But for legal and economic reasons, companies continue to make their users accountable for making and protecting their own passwords so that the server and service owners can't be blamed for giving access to the wrong person.

So how you prove who you are, how you sign up, make passwords, retrieve lost passwords, change accounts, etc. is in YOUR slippery hands.

But you only have a problem if you're careless with your accounts, share them, get phished, click on something you shouldn't, get malware on your system, or any part of your communications are hijacked. So no problem because that like NEVER happens! (Note: see every major criminal hack in the last 5 years and a book on sarcasm).

So yes, the current scheme of login and password that we all know and suffer under is a careful blend of legal deniability, fiscal sensibility, and a hefty pinch of what most parents of the world call "not thinking things through". You don't ask regular people to make irregular passwords. But it's done all the time so, you still need to know how to make unbeatable passwords and protect them.

Hashed Passwords and Salts

Once everyone discovered that storing passwords in plain text was a bad, really, really bad idea, some smart folks came up with a better system. Instead of keeping passwords lying around in plain text, let's encrypt them. The problems with encryption are the computing power required to encrypt and decrypt the password, and safely storing the encryption keys. Ha ha, got your keys! Now we have ALL your passwords.

Next, some smart folks came up with the idea of using a one-way **hash** algorithm on a password to create a hash string. This hash value can't (in theory) be reproduced through reverse engineering, hence the name "one-way." Easy, right?

Hashes (MD5, SHA-1, SHA-2 and SHA-3)

A hash is a mathematical formula that uses a password and sometimes random data (a **salt**) to return a single value. Think of a hash as a locksmith creating a key to fit one lock. The locksmith uses unique materials and special tools to make each key so that only one key will ever fit that one lock. This **hash key** is built using the password as part of the material and some added information (the salt) to make the rest of the key. The hash key or **hash string** will only match one particular lock. If you try to create a duplicate key, the fake key won't match because only one key will ever fit that one lock. It's pretty tight.

Let's try this another way. Take a can of colored paints, blue, green, red, yellow, brown, white, purple and mix some of each paint into a small jar. Don't worry about how much of each paint you add, just pour, mix, repeat. Whatever color that jar becomes with all those colors mixed in, is fairly original. It would be difficult to duplicate this process and make the exact same color.

Now, let's repeat this exercise with a bucket full of sand. In that bucket each grain of sand is slightly different from the next, and there are millions and millions of pieces of sand in there. This means getting another bucket full of the exact size, color, and shape of each piece of sand in that original bucket would be almost impossible. When you are done with your first bucket of sand, throw it into the ocean. Now, try and locate an exact duplicate bucket of that first sand batch at another beach located on the other side of the world. A hash value is almost (yes, almost) impossible to repeat ever again.

Those grains of sand or exact mixes of color are what are used to formulate an answer, not the sand or paint themselves. If one grain of sand in the new bucket is slightly different from the original, the calculations will be wrong. Any one change to the data will result in a completely different calculation answer: The lock will not open.

Since nothing has to be encrypted and decrypted, it's easier to calculate a hash value when a user types in a password. Instead of looking up the user's password, the password's hash value is calculated and compared to a stored hash.

Salt

The random bits of data that are added to the hash algorithm, like a key for computations, is called the **salt**. A salt can be used to help create the hash value when combined with the original password, since it adds additional levels of complexity to the answer key. All this hashing and salting creates a one-way hash value. A salt is usually a string of random data from 48 to 128 bits long. The longer the salt, the higher the level of complexity and difficulty to crack.

Using a salt with the hash value makes many password attack methods impractical, such as the good old dictionary attack, otherwise know as a brute force attack. More on these attacks later in this lesson.

One of the attack techniques mitigated by salts is **rainbow tables**. With this technique an attacker pre-generates huge lists of hashes. In order to add complexity and prevent this attack, you can generate a specific salt for each user (so that an attacker would need to pre-compute a rainbow table for each user) and store a part of the salt in a different location than the passwords (so the attacker needs to compromise more systems to get enough information to generate rainbow tables.

Feed Your Head: Understanding Linux Passwords

A password salt is a string that is added on to a user's password before it is encrypted. This string could be anything, the user's username, their email address, the exact time the user signed up, or something completely random.

The point of a password salt is to make a password more secure by making it much harder to crack. It does this by making the password longer, and by making each password hash different from every other, even if the password is the same.

For example, if the password is "password", the final hash would be calculated from:

MD5 ["random salt"+"password]

so even if someone else used that same password, their salt would be different, which would result in a different password hash. This way, if the attacker cracks a password, he wouldn't be able to find every other user with the same password because their hashes would be different.

Once the hacker finds out what the salt is, this is no longer the case. The attacker can edit any dictionary or brute force password cracker code to add the salt to the current word before running it through the hash function. The attacker can now run normal password lists and brute force attacks as if the salt wasn't even there.

This can also applied on a larger scale. If the attacker found out that the salt was the user's username, he could easily automate a password cracker by editing the code to attach the user's username to the password. So as you can see, it is important to create good salts and store them as securely as possible.

Random Salt/ Unique Salts

So which is better, having random generated salts, or unique salts like your username or email address? It depends on how you store it. If it is in the same database as your username and password hash, then it doesn't matter if it's random or unique, because it's being stored either way.

Once the hacker gets access to the database and dumps the username/password database, to figure out what the salt is, all he would need to try attaching every stored value (username, email, name, etc.) to a possible password until he cracked the password. He would then know what the salt was for every other user. The attacker could also just choose to try and crack the password hash as is, and if successful he would see the salt and password in plaintext. The attacker would then compare the plaintext with the database values under that user and see where it matches up, finding the salt. This would probably take much longer or wouldn't work depending on how long the salt and password combination is.

This would be a different situation if the salt was stored in a different server because if the attacker had access to one database, he might not have access to the other. In this case, using a random salt would make sense because the attacker would still be able to guess a unique salt like a username, but not a random hash stored elsewhere.

For even greater security, in addition to using a salt that is stored in the database, you could add to it in the actual source code of the register/login script. This way, the attacker would need to have access to both the database and the source code to be able to get the salt.

Crackstation has a good guide to proper password hashing:

https://crackstation.net/hashing-security.htm

Linux Password Cracking

Boot to a CD, DVD or USB Linux that includes John the Ripper. As always we recommend the Fedora Security Spin.

Log in as root.

Open a terminal. You're going to need to mount the root partition of the computer's hard disk. On most newer computers it will be /dev/sda1, though you may need to examine your /dev directory. The disk could be hda instead of sda, and you may not be using partition 1, maybe it's 2 or 3. Be ready to experiment. The critical commands you'll run are these:

        md /mnt/harddisk

(This is to make a directory that you can mount or attach the hard disk partition to.)

        mount /dev/sda1 /mnt/harddisk

(to mount the sda1 partition of the hard disk to the directory you created, so you can access it)

        unshadow /mnt/harddisk/etc/passwd /mnt/xyz/etc/shadow >crackpassword

(file name crackpassword is created)

        john crackpassword

(loads the carckpassword file)

        john -show crackpassword

(outputs the cracked password - eventually)

Sample output:

        user1:letmein:1002:1002:user1,,,/home/user1:/bin/bash
        1 password cracked

Key Derivation Functions

A step forward in hash functions are **key derivation functions**. These are used to derive keys from a string, a salt and a (big) number of iterations in a formula something like this:

DK=KDF(Key, Salt, Iterations)

where DK is the derived key, KDF is the key derivation function, Key is the original key or password, Salt is the cryptographic salt and Iterations refers to the number of times the subfunction is run.

The whole point is to make hash generation slow. "Fast" hash algorithms let brute-force and dictionary attacks run wild; slow algorithms make them too slow to be practical in many cases.

Super Duper Complex Cryptography

Take a deep breath and turn off your cellphone for this next section. We will do our best to avoid giving you nightmares or headaches about complex mathematics. If you want, you can just skip this section if you scare easily or are prone to fits of rage.

Cryptology means altering information or data to make it incomprehensible and unreadable unless you possess some secret knowledge. One of the ways we do this is encryption.

Back when passwords were encrypted, there were lots of places to get attacked. The effectiveness of encryption, usually described as its **strength**, ranges from very weak to extremely robust.

At the weakest, passwords were simply **encoded**. This produces a password that is not readable directly, but, given the key, can easily be translated using a computer, pen and paper, or a plastic decoder ring from a cereal box. An example of this is the **ROT13 cypher**. ROT13 replaces every letter in a text with the letter that is 13 places away from it in the alphabet. For example "ABC" becomes "NOP."

Even when using algorithms that can more accurately be called encryption, the encryption is weak if the key used to generate it is weak. Using ROT13 as an example, with the 13 place differential as the key, then ROT13 has an extremely weak key. ROT13 can be strengthened by using a different key. You could use ROT10, replacing each letter with the one ten places forward, or you could use ROT-2, replacing each letter with the one two places before it. You could strengthen it even more, by varying the differential, such as ROTpi, where the first letter is shifted 3 places; the second, 1 place; the third, 4 places; the fourth, 1 place; and so on, using pi (3.14159265...) to provide a constantly varying differential.

Because of these possible variations, when you are encrypting any type of information, you must be sure that you are using a reliable method of encryption and that the key – your contribution to the encryption – will provide you with a robust result.

You must also remember that a good system of encryption is useless without good passwords, just as good passwords are useless without good encryption.

I Don't Get It

So basically, encryption is a two-way mechanism. You start with a plaintext written letter, encrypt it to cyphertext and send it to whomever you want. They receive it, decipher it with the key you gave them earlier and they read your original plaintext written letter.

Hackers realized years ago that to keep passwords really secure, you couldn't store them encrypted, because given enough time (and computing power) you can **crack** (decipher) them. So instead of encrypting passwords, systems started to use **hashing**.

Hashing involves taking something (a file, a password, a document) and running a series of operations on it, leaving you with a series of characters called a **digest** or a **hash**. Hashing is a **one way function**, because unlike encryption, what you get at the end of the process is not reversible. This means that starting from the digest or hash, you will never be able to re-create the original data. (In theory.) But the same data, using the same hashing algorithm, will always generate the same digest. Not only that, but if you change so much as one letter in a 1000 page document, the digest will be completely different.

Exercises

4.7   Here is a list of fruits encoded using the ROT13 cypher. Try to decode them:

   a) nccyr

   b) benatr

   c) yrzba

   d) jngrezryba

   e) gbzngb

4.8   Is there a web page that will allow you to decode the ROT13 encoded words automatically?

4.9 There are a lot of things that are called encryption, but many of these are really just simple encoding methods. True encryption requires a **key** in order to encode or decode. Of the following systems, which ones are true methods of encryption and which ones are simple encoding?

a) Twofish

b) MIME

c) RSA

d) CAST

e) AES

f) BASE64

g) IDEA

h) TripleDES

i) ROT13

j) TLS

Game On: Sucker's Bet

Jace was hungry for those three cookies but she was even more thrilled about showing Mokoa how much he didn't know about passwords. In a deliberate attempt to hide the plate of treats, she moved his laptop in front of the dish on the counter, a decoy as she planned her assault on the snack.

Jace started her next series of password cracking moves by rebooting Mokoa's computer to her USB drive. His BIOS allowed for USB bootable devices so Katana popped up in the Linux environment from her drive. Jace mounted the laptop's hard drive and she was able to recover all available hash values in a few seconds.

Mokoa asked, "So what. Now all you have is the hashes of my passwords. You don't know the actual passwords 'cause I don't store the passwords on my computer. How do you expect to get my password from that gibberish?"

Jace grinned back and replied, "You're right: a hash digest works in only one direction. So like maybe you're painting your room or whatever, so you go to the paint store with a sample of the paint you want to match. You're not trying to get the exact same paint, just one that matches."

Squirming in his chair, unsure of his next question, he asked, "Okay, but you can't match passwords like you can with paint. The matches have to be exact for passwords to work. How are you planning on finding that?"

The hacker placed her hand on Mokoa's shoulder. "Relax, dude. I'm going to show you a few ways," she said in a calming voice.

"Okay, let's forget about hash values for a moment. You suck at picking passwords. No, you do. Everybody sucks at making up passwords. We use easy-to-remember things; we add the same two numbers to the end of our passwords, one and two. We capitalize the first digit of every password. If we add any additional characters to a password, it's almost always going to be either an explanation point or a question mark. People use the same password for everything. And so do you, I'll bet."

Mokoa frowned at the idea that he sucked at picking passwords. For a diversion he fished out his cell phone to check it. Jace used that split second to grab a cookie and scarf it down without Mokoa noticing.

She swiped crumbs off her face and continued, "You seen those lists of the worst passwords? Like 12345 or password? Sites like Splash Data (http://splashdata.com) do 'em every year. Then there's lists of 'plains,' plain-text passwords and their hash values. Any computer can run through like thousands of hashes in a few seconds and match passwords against a hash list. Nobody cracks passwords by trying to log in. It's done offline with a hash list."

Mokoa blinked. Jace continued, "So there's a bunch of password cracking programs out there, like Hashcat (http://hashcat.net/hashcat/). Hashcat doesn't come with any lists but it does have a huge collection of rules to choose from. So you provide the list and Hashcat provides the passwords."

Mokoa looked at his screen and then looked away, obviously re-thinking his passwords. Jace reached behind the screen again and popped a cookie in her mouth.

"Most of the really good password crackers use graphics cards GPUs 'cause they're fast like crazy. But, when you think about it, all you really need is one password to get inside a network. Once your password's compromised, it's only a matter of time before every account you have has been hacked because...."

Mokoa interrupted, "Because you used the same password for every account."

"Bingo," Jace said. "Now hand me your cell phone for a second." As he hesitated Jace grabbed the last cookie and shoved it into her mouth.

"What are you going to do with my cellphone," he asked, obviously afraid of her answer, but he handed her the phone.

"Just wait and see," she said, pecking away on his tiny screen. She handed the phone back to him without showing him what she'd done.

Jace continued, "I gotta big advantage: I know you. I know you very well. I know what you like and hate, your hobbies, your birthday and all kinds of other handy clues what your password might be. That's how crackers tailor their password searches. Brute force cracking is okay for passwords up to six letters, but complex passwords take more time and more CPU. If you have a really good word list then brute force can pay off, but it takes lots of work to build a good word list. With hashes, you can compare them against the list you have. You're looking for whatever combination of characters can produce a given hash value. You're matching one against another and once you find a word that creates that hash value, you now know the password. It's just like matching paint."

Jace looked at Mokoa and asked, "Clear as mud or do you understand a little bit of this stuff?"

"No, no. I get it," Mokoa leaned back and smiled. "I also get that you are way past the 90 seconds you were given to crack my password. You haven't even gotten close to getting into my account. You lose, I win. Hand over the cookies."

Jace sighed and lowered her head. "I cracked it a while ago. Check your cell phone. I even sent you a text with a time and date on it to prove when I cracked it."

Shocked, he pulled out his phone and saw the message. The text was his password and it was sent four minutes ago. "Alright, good job. You win. How 'bout we split the cookies," he offered.

Jace closed the laptop to expose the empty cookie plate. "Too bad, so sad. Never make a bet if you don't already know the outcome," she said as she slipped past him and headed out the pet shop door.

Game Over

Password Cracking

Password cracking for anything other than stuff you own is against the law. If it's your password, then it's your information. Once you password protect something, and then forget your password, you are stuck. Or in another common scenario, you're taking over management of a network and didn't get all the password information from the last admin. This is where password recovery becomes really useful.

Sometimes, for research or analysis, experts crack giant lists of password hashes, which is called **hashcracking**. What they're trying to find are **plains**: plain-text passwords. Methods for cracking fall into just a few categories. These include:

Use the (Brute) Force

This is one of the most misused terms in password cracking. While in a generic sense you can say this term means trying millions of passwords until you find the one you're looking for, that's not accurate in our world. (Show people how 1337 you are by knowing what it really is.) Actually, brute-force attacks try every possible combination in the keyspace, or at least as many as it takes to find the password. They don't start with a list; they generate all the permutations on the fly. This means that brute-force attacks are very thorough on the one hand, but can take a very long time to run on the other. That's why experienced password crackers will try brute-forcing passwords of up to seven or eight characters in lower-case only, then switch to other attacks for longer and more complex passwords. You'd think people wouldn't use such simple passwords – but about ten percent of them did in a 2013 experiment by ArsTechnica.

In a brute force attack, you are basically taking a library of words, numbers, or characters and trying to match each one against the actual password. When you are looking for your socks, you can always find one clean sock but you can never find the other matching sock. So, you look through your room picking up every sock you can find and comparing it to the one clean sock you have. You are thinking to yourself, "is it this one, is it this one, is it that one" as you stumble to locate the other matching sock. Brute force works the same way, it just doesn't smell as bad.

As mentioned earlier, humans tend to be creatures of habit. Users will make passwords that are easy to remember. Often, those passwords are common words found in a dictionary. Brute force uses several libraries to compare against the encrypted password, looking for a match. This type of attack works well if you are looking for your own lost password and you just needed a hint.

The key to success in using this attack is to use as large and as many different types of word lists (libraries). A good brute force attack may only uncover some of the digits in the password, yet that may be enough for you to guess the rest of the password. This type of attack is called a dictionary attack since you are using words found in a dictionary.

Don't be fooled by the simplicity of this attack method. It may take up all of your computing resources and a tremendous amount of time before a match is found, if one is found at all. Be prepared to use another computer while the brute force attack is ongoing. Across the Internet you can find tools that will automate this process for you. This may be kindly of them, or it may be a ruse to crack that password for themselves.

Exercises

4.10 First you'll need a **hashdump** file, preferably a huge dump of millions of hashes for you to gleefully crack with your friends. Get lots of potato chips.

You're going to get a truly epic dump of password hashes courtesy of every user of Linkedin in 2012. (Thanks, everyone.) Use your search engine skills to locate the file:

we suggest a search along the lines of "Linkedin hashdump and passwords" if that doesn't make it too obvious.

Download the file. Unzip it. Put it someplace sensible, somewhere that you can remember.

4.11 Now you need a tool that can put that hash dump to use. Go to http://hashcat.net/hashcat/ and download **hashcat**. This is a serious professional tool, and you're expected to figure it out for yourself. Amazingly, this is in fact possible. On the same page, scroll to the bottom to the Help section and follow the Video link to a video site. There are excellent step-by-step tutorials that you can explore at your leisure, but for now look for one that's under five minutes in the first page of results. One we'll suggest is "Using Hashcat to Bruteforce Encrypted Hashes" on Youtube, which gives you a good example of the syntax:

```
hashcat-cli.exe -a 3 -m 0 -o cracked.txt -n 1 --bf-pw-min=2 --bf-pw-max=15
--bf-cs-buf=0123456789 hash.txt
where -a is the attack type, in this case 3 for brute force,
-m is the hash mode, in this case 0 for MD5,
-o is the output file for cracked passwords, in this case cracked.txt,
-n is the number of threads, in this case 1,
- -bf-pw-min=2 means that we're setting the minimum password length to two
characters,
- -bf-pw-max=15 means we're looking for up to 15 characters,
- -bf-sc-buf=0123456789 means that the character space buffer holds the
characters 0-9,
and hash.txt is the name of the file with all the hashes. Substitute the
names of the real files you got in the above exercise.
```

You can get more information, like the numbers for different attack types and has modes, with the command:

```
hashcat-cli.exe -help
```

See if you can crack some hashes. Particularly try different lists of characters in the character set buffer for lots of fun revelations.

4.12 Do you have a hot nVidia or AMD video card? The requirements are pretty strict, but you may be able to use **oclHashcat**. Visit http://hashcat.net/oclhashcat/ and see if you can use it. If you can, you'll instantly leap to cracking at the rate of millions of attempts per second. And if you have a lust for sheer horsepower, this technique becomes addictive really fast. You can crack 90% of this list, with research.

Dictionary attacks

These run through a series of possible dictionary words until one works as a password. This is slow for a different reason than brute force: each word in the dictionary has to be hashed, then compared to the hash you're cracking. Dictionary files, or **word lists**, are available all over the Internet, though the quality varies hugely. A simple word list might just list words alphabetically, but the probability of letters or words showing up isn't the same as alphabetical order, so these lists are always slow. An optimized or custom word list will put more-likely words first, meaning that the solution will probably be found more quickly. Master hashcrackers build their own word lists and guard them jealously. You won't find many or any of these online. You'll have to make friends with somebody who has them. But choose your friends carefully: some people are researchers (hackers) and some people are criminals (crackers). Don't learn the difference the hard way.

As a hacker or security professional you will need a fairly decent set of software tools, scripts and hardware to do your job properly. The interesting part of computer security is that hackers openly share their tools across the Internet, yet security companies charge big bucks for their security tools and knowledge. Open Source software is provided to anyone for free as long as proper credit is given and the software is not commercialized in anyway. Pretty cool, huh?

Exercises

4.13 Now you need some word lists. Openwall offers several sample word lists at http://download.openwall.net/pub/word lists/. Go there and download the all.gz file, which contains (you guessed it) all of the word lists.

Linux and OSX can unzip Gzipped files natively. In Windows you'll need an add-on compression tool like 7zip (http://www.7-zip.org/). Get it if you need it. Unzip all.gz and put the output in a logical place.

4.14 Now you need a tool that can put those word lists to use. This time we're going to use John the Ripper, so you can get experience with more than one tool. Remember that Hashcat could do the job too.

We'll start with software password crackers. **John the Ripper** at http://www.openwall.com/john/ is at the top of the list for its success and longevity. John works on several platforms (across platforms) such as UNIX, Windows, OpenVMS, and BeOS. If you build a live CD or bootable USB drive, you must include John because it's that good. Trust us. John is an Open Source package and has been worked on over the years by teams of volunteers.

Get it. Install it. If you're using the Fedora Security Spin, you've already got it.

4.15 Open your new friend John and see what you need to do to crack passwords from your list.

4.16 There are other things you can do with John and handy accessories like Pyrit and coWPAtty. Search for and find the article titled "Apocalyps of Passwords" (yes, it really is spelled like that). Read it. Can you follow the instructions?

Somewhere Over the Rainbow

How do you speed up a dictionary attack? Well, how about pre-hashing all those dictionary files? That would sort of make sense, until you remember that there are lots of different hashing algorithms out there. What you really need to do is hash each password with several different algorithms, and store the results in a table with a column for each algorithm. These tables, with the plain and the hashes of different fixed lengths, looked like a rainbow to somebody somewhere, and that's how we got the name. **Rainbow tables** are an example of **space/time tradeoff**. In this case, the tradeoff is between huge (and we mean really huge) use of disk space, to save huge amounts of time during actual cracking runs.

In practice, creating rainbow tables of entire word lists is impractical precisely because of the issue of file size: you'll fill up that terabyte drive fast. So hashcrackers do something different, something very, very smart. The crack the hash by cracking small parts of it at a time, then assembling the parts. This is wildly clever and intensely mathematical. If you are a hard-core math geek you are gonna love this stuff.

One logical attack is to look for repeated values in calculations. Using a hash (with salt) the word "Stun" could look like **dr23 n9n2 8v84 2lwi**. So, why not look for a pattern in other hash calculations to see if you can find a match?

Rainbow tables do a nice trick. Instead of looking for a whole password (or whatever it is you're trying to decrypt), rainbow tables let you look for fragments or pieces of passwords. Rainbow tables aren't exactly tables; they are a collection of columns in which each column uses a different reduction function. If you assigned each a color you could think of the columns as a curve, or a rainbow. Hence the name rainbow tables. The whole idea is that if the calculated values of any two "colors" matches, you've found part of the password.

From a mathematical perspective, try and wrap your mind around a simple formula of

```
v+x-4= 162
```

both v and x could be any combination of numbers as long as the answer equals 162.

The rainbow tables already have hash values computed and any input you provide (to crack a password) is matched against each column (reducing the values) until a perfect match is found. As we saw with "Stun" above, the hash calculation would look like this: **dr23 n9n2 8v84 2lwi**. If you were to apply this dr23 n9n2 8v84 2lwi string into a rainbow table automated lookup generator, every two digits are analyzed and reduced to find a matching character. While this lookup is occurring, each column is reducing your input, thus speeding up the match finding process. Simple stuff, right?

All the rainbow tables are doing is looking for the answer v+x-4= 162. The v and the x values are the unknown factors and the tables have already been calculated to find that type of answer, just on a massive scale.

Since hash values are one-way, it is impossible to reverse engineer any hash string and expect to get a correct answer. Think of a hash calculation as a door that only opens in one direction and traffic can only flow in that same direction. It is highly likely that hash values will be the same somewhere along the way and that is how rainbow tables operate. They compare hash calculations that you provided against a massive collection of predetermined hash values. As the two digit set moves through the table, each column reduces the answer until a match is found.

Exercises

4.17 Rainbow Tables

Get some rainbow Tables from http://ophcrack.sourceforge.net/tables.php for Windows XP, Vista or 7.

4.18 Ophcrack

Ophcrack is another valuable password cracker that needs to be in your toolbox. It is an open source project that also works across platform, including Macs. Ophcrack is mainly available as a live CD but has a large selection of tools within the overall package. Ophcrack can conduct a SAM dump (collect passwords from a Windows system), conduct a brute force attack and even perform a rainbow table analysis. Ophcrak is available for Windows and Linux at http://ophcrack.sourceforge.net/download.php.

1. Boot a Windows system to a Linux forensics USB stick that contains Ophcrack.

2. Mount the Windows hard disk.

3. Navigate to WINDOWS/system32/config/. You will see two files: SAM and System. Copy both files.

4. Create a new folder on your desktop and paste the files inside.

5. Open a terminal and run the command

   ophcrack

   The Ophcrack GUI will open.

6. Click Load and select Encrypted SAM. Select the directory where you saved the SAM file. Now it will load and display the list of user accounts.

7. Remove all other accounts except the target admin account.

8. Unzip the rainbow table: tables_xp_free_small.zip or tables_vista_free.zip or the appropriate file.

9. Click the Table button in Ophcrack . Now it will ask you to select the table. Select the appropriate table and click the install button. Now browse to the rainbow table directory you just unzipped and choose tables_xp_free_small or tables_vista_free etc. Now click Ok.

10. Click the Crack button. Wait for a while. Ophcrack is one of the fastest cracking tools around, so it won't take too much time.

11. Now the cracked password will be displayed.

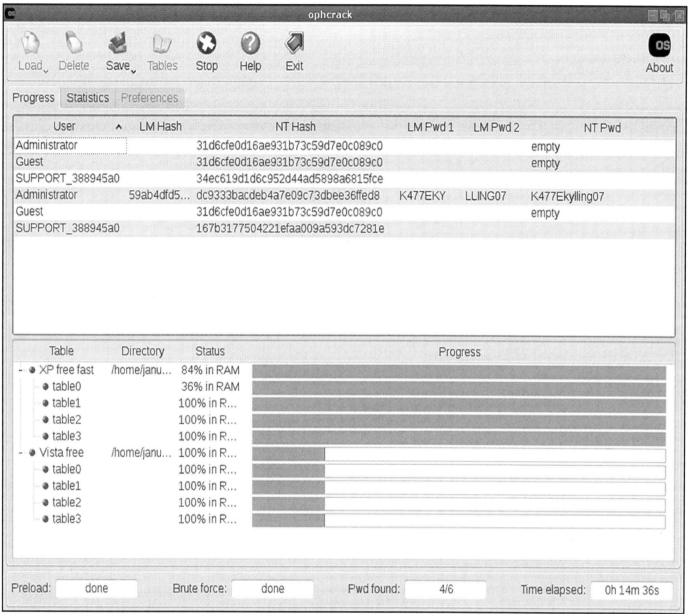

Figure 4.1: *Ophcrack*

L0phtcrack

L0phtcrack is a powerful commercial password auditing tool. Help can be found on the official website at http://www.l0phtcrack.com/help/using.html. See if you can afford it.

Combinator Attacks

Unfortunately, rainbow tables have a weakness: they're easily defeated when systems use a salt. We'll talk about those below, but the gist is this: when the user creates a password, the system also creates a random salt (a string of a few letters to add to the password), combines password and salt, and only then creates the hash. Every user's salt is unique to them. The salt can be stored unencrypted in the same table as the password hashes, in theory. At least that's the way they used to do it. Obviously it's way too easy to steal both the hash and the salt, if they're in the same table, so it's a much better idea to store the salts in a separate table, or in a separate database, or on a separate machine. In any case, the added salt makes the original password much harder to derive from the hash, effectively defeating rainbow table attacks. Fooey.

Okay, you broke our rainbow tables? Fine, we'll do something else smart. We specialize in smart. How about we try something like this:

1. First, we've all got machines with powerhouse graphics cards, right? Good: now,

2. Run a brute-force attack for lower-case-only passwords up to six characters, and

3. Repeat for upper-case-only passwords up to six characters. This lets us keep passwords of six characters or less out of our word lists; brute force can test literally all possible combinations.

4. Then run a dictionary attack using, of course, highly optimized word lists. Let this run for at most an hour, so we capture the most likely passwords.

5. Next, let's use that same word list again, but truncate all the words down to seven characters or less, then put a 1 at the end. Try again with a 2 at the end. Try again with a bang (!) at the end. Run all these trials only until cracked-password output slows down.

6. Chop the words in the list down to six and try brute force again with up to two digits or special characters, then three. If you've got a hot graphics card try four, otherwise at the three or four digit length switch to digits only (no special characters). Appending the output of a brute-force attack to the words in a list makes this a **combinator attack**.

7. Transform every password in the word list by making its first character upper-case. This is where people put upper-case letters: at the front of the password. Taking advantage of this kind of pattern turns a brute-force or dictionary attack into a **mask attack**, an especially deadly attack that reduces the keyspace dramatically so that cracking happens much more quickly.

We can run each of these attacks for only as long as they produce lots of plains quickly, then jump to the next attack. We want lots of plains today, not all the plains next month. We're doing research, or we're in a competition, right?

Location, Location, Location

Say you're having a security contest with some friends. If you have physical access to your target's computer, **try looking around:** passwords are often taped to the bottom of keyboards, under mouse pads, posted on personal bulletin boards, in calendars or daily planners, wherever is handy. People tend to post their passwords in plain view but try to be tricky by writing the password backwards. It is not that people are lazy, they just to make their lives as uncomplicated as possible.

There are two commonly used methods to crack hash values in Windows. The first one is an injection using Local Security Authority Subsystem Service (LSASS) and the other is taking a direct reading off of the registry using SAM/System. LSASS reads the hash directly from memory, while SAM reads the local registry hives. There are other methods that can be used to gather hash values but LSASS and registry reads have a higher probability of success without revealing the attackers tracks or location. Then the attacker can research and crack those hashes at his leisure off-line. That's especially handy because the attacker can gather several (if not all) the hash strings in a single breach.

Network-based Password Cracking

What about those times when you don't have a password hashdump, but need to recover the password to a database, web application or some other online service? This is when you need a **network password cracking** tool.

THC Hydra

A speedy network authentication cracker which supports plenty of different services, Hydra is at https://www.thc.org/thc-hydra/. When you need to brute force crack a remote authentication service, Hydra is often the tool of choice. It can perform speedy dictionary assaults against more than 30 protocols, including telnet, ftp, http, https, smb, several databases and many more.

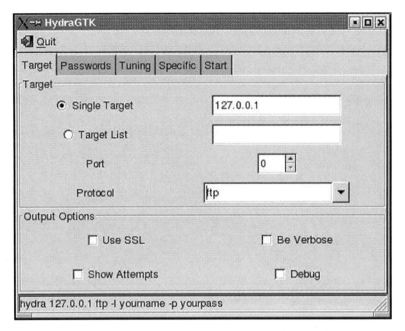

Figure 4.2: *Selecting a target in Hydra*

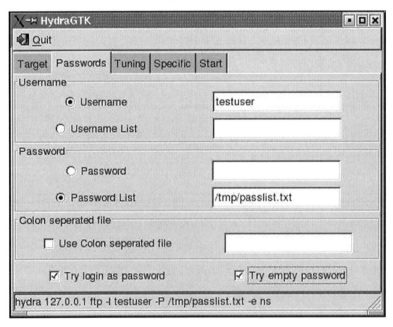

Figure 4.3: *Setting up Username and Password lists in Hydra*

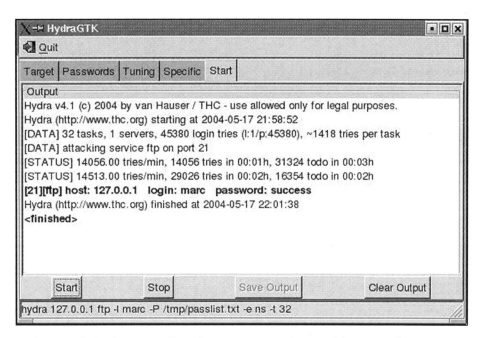

Figure 4.4: *The results of a password cracking run in Hydra*

Wireless Password Cracking

Aircrack-ng - http://www.aircrack-ng.org/

Once upon a time there was **Aircrack**, an open-source wireless security testing suite. It was good, but this field changes fast, so along came the next-generation suite (which is a fork, or split-off project, of the Aircrack project) called **Aircrack-ng**.

Aircrack-ng contains several tools: **airodump-ng** (a packet capture program), **aireplay-ng** (a packet injection program), **aircrack-ng** (for static WEP and WPA-PSK cracking), and **airdecap-ng** [decrypts WEP/WPA capture files]. The suite can recover a 40-bit through 512-bit WEP keys once encrypted packets have been gathered. It can also assault WPA or WPA2 networks using advanced cryptographic methods or by brute force.

It needs a wireless network interface controller with a driver that supports raw monitoring mode (injection), and can sniff 802.11a, 802.11b and 802.11g traffic. There are versions for Linux and Windows; the Linux version has been ported for **OpenWrt** (a popular open-source wireless access point operating system) as well as the Android, Zaurus and Maemo platforms.

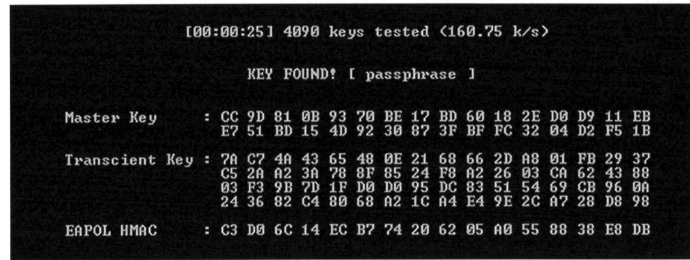

```
C:\aircrack-ng-0.4.2-win\bin>aircrack-ng.exe -a 2 -w dict capture2.cap
Opening capture2.cap
Read 607 packets.

   #  BSSID              ESSID                    Encryption

   1  00:06:25:BF:64:99  cuckoo                   WPA (1 handshake)

Choosing first network as target.
```

Figure 4.5: *Cracking a WEP key with aircrack-ng*

```
          [00:00:25] 4090 keys tested (160.75 k/s)

                  KEY FOUND! [ passphrase ]

   Master Key      : CC 9D 81 0B 93 70 BE 17 BD 60 18 2E D0 D9 11 EB
                     E7 51 BD 15 4D 92 30 87 3F BF FC 32 04 D2 F5 1B

   Transcient Key : 7A C7 4A 43 65 48 0E 21 68 66 2D A8 01 FB 29 37
                     C5 2A A2 3A 78 8F 85 24 F8 A2 26 03 CA 62 43 88
                     03 F3 9B 7D 1F D0 D0 95 DC 83 51 54 69 CB 96 0A
                     24 36 82 C4 80 68 A2 1C A4 E4 9E 2C A7 28 D8 98

   EAPOL HMAC      : C3 D0 6C 14 EC B7 74 20 62 05 A0 55 88 38 E8 DB
```

Figure 4.6: *A successful WEP key crack*

Exercises

4.19 Are you familiar with null-byte on WonderHowTo.com? Get familiar. Go here:

http://null-byte.wonderhowto.com/how-to/hack-wi-fi-cracking-wpa2-psk-passwords-using-aircrack-ng-0148366/

Read this step-by-step tutorial. If your instructor can supply a wireless access point as a lab target, or you have your own, see if you can crack its key.

4.20 This article mentions another tool: coWPAtty. Find the linked article and read it. How does coWPAtty compare with aircrack-ng?

Cracked Up

For serious password cracking you will need some additional tools. One of these tools is your average graphics card, known as a GPU for Graphics Processor Unit. These cards are designed for repetitive tasks unlike a CPU, which is designed to all kinds of tasks. Even though your computer, smartphone, tablet and other devices have GPUs built into them, those chips are unlikely to be programmable by the user. They are locked chips that only accelerate the graphics for that device. The type of GPU needed to crack passwords (or mine bitcoins) are higher end gamer cards. A couple of these cards in a computer can crack passwords dozens of times faster but also costs more money.

You will want to take a look at either nVidia G-Force or Radeon cards made by AMD. They are similar in speed and price with best results obtained by using several mid range cards in tandem. Performance increases significantly when multiple cards are used instead of a single high end GPU. Some experts argue that the AMD cards are superior to the G-Force cards based on the usage of integer instructions in Radeon GPUs. It will be up to you to research which card offers the best password cracking benchmarks if you are going that route. This also applies to the device that you intend to use for your work.

Computers have ample computing power because they have plenty of power available. This isn't the case when it comes to laptops, smartphones, tablets or minicomputers like Raspberry Pis and Beagle Bone Boards. In these cases, you will need to do your homework to locate devices that already have these chips installed. Minicomputers allow you to add on capes, shields, or boards where you can customize your own GPU but power will still be a major consideration. High end gaming laptops have this same issue because they are built for power and speed, not portability. It is the same with any device running a graphic or computing intensive program, you will need plenty of juice. This can be overcome by having a hot swappable battery or a portable battery charger like the Anker. That thing can jump start a car.

Older computers can make great password cracking machines with a few low cost modifications. First of all, you will need to replace the power supply with a much larger one because we've been talking about power for the past three paragraphs. Next, the motherboard will need to handle several fullsize graphics cards, at least three, more if possible. You won't need to worry about the CPU or other hardware because this machine will only be used to crack passwords or mine bitcoins. Heat and ventilation will be another consideration but that can be taken care of by drilling holes in the case, adding cheap fans, clearing out unnecessary hardware, or installing a liquid cooling system. Above all, keep the computer in an area that has good airflow.

If your computer motherboard can't fit the GPU cards, you can always build an additional box (old shoebox or a wooden crate) and add PCI extension cables along with power cords to link them to your machine. Linux OS will be your best bet thanks to the highly customizable interfaces available but Windows will work too.

Hardware may sound unlikely for cracking passwords, but there are amazing ways to use devices in other ways. Video cards were designed to display better graphics than your CPU can, and free up the CPU for other tasks. An interesting thing happened on the way to better video performance: a group figured out that NVidia Cuda and certain ATI Radeon graphics cards would crack passwords. Of course, this required designing software for the purpose of hacking passwords, but it sounded like a great challenge.

Certain video cards provide amazing data acceleration to break strong encryption. A video card really is just one data accelerator after all. With a little tweaking and fine tuning, hackers have stacked (parallel) bunches of video cards together. Students at MIT brought this data acceleration to a whole new level when they added the computing power of the Sony Playstation. You read it right. Using a parallel pattern (like stacking columns of bricks instead of one single column), the students demonstrated a machine that could crack several encryption algorithms that were once thought too complex to break.

This is what hacking is really about, taking technology and making that technology better or creating something entirely new out of it. Real hackers are more like inventors, always trying to tweak this or that and building new ideas or gadgets out of other electronic or digital parts. Too often the word "hacker" is used when people mean "criminal." If a carpenter breaks into your house with a hammer, is he a carpenter or a criminal?

The Soft Side

Thanks to the ever increasing computing power of technology, password cracking has gotten much easier. People are often asked to provide an email address to create their username, which makes the first part of hacking an account that much simpler. Since most people use the same email account for all their work, knowing one email account means you probably know the username for every account that person has. Having the username, your next step is to figure out their password. We've talked about human conditions and the flaws of passwords where most people tend to use the same for every account they have. The average person has twenty five accounts.

One of the best software programs out there for password recovery is **oclHashcat** available at http://hashcat.net/oclhashcat/. This tool runs on both Linux and Windows and is aimed at either AMD or nVidia's graphics cards. Besides having control over almost every aspect of decrypting passwords, it also provides a watchdog to ensure you don't fry your GPU due to over temperature. Hashcat rightfully claims to be the fastest GPU enabled password cracker that is free. There are limitations such as it cannot crack Truecrypt 6.0 or above but other than that, the software has an amazing track record of recovering lost passwords.

New hash lists can be found dumped at Pastebin.com and other sites. The largest collection of plain text passwords was from a 2009 breach of an online gaming company called Rockyou.com. This is a database of 14.3 million passwords and can be found on several password collection sites. Hash lists have already been run against this massive collection and you can usually find both the password and MD5 hash list on the same site. If you look around long enough you will find over 100 million cracked passwords available online. One of them is probably yours.

Exercises

4.21 Do some research into the pros and cons of LSASS versus gathering hash strings using registry hives. Which method would you use if the target server was running Windows 10 server? Hint: DEFCON.

4.22 If you had established a typical user account on the target server, what steps should you take before attempting either recommended method for obtaining hash values from a windows server? How about a UNIX platform?

4.23 Ready for a curve-ball? **Novell** is still operating on a small amount of servers out there. You just might come across a target running "Groupwise." Novell was the DoD standard for secure servers back in the early 1990's before Windows NT and Enterprise. Research **Groupwise** and see if those servers use a hash salt or if they have another procedure to authenticate users, without using a hash.

4.24 While you are at it, try and locate an organization/server using Novell software (besides Novell) on the Internet. What type of industry is that organization in?

Build a Great Password

The best passwords:

- •cannot be found in a dictionary (any language dictionary)

- •contain numbers, letters and those odd symbols on top of the number keys

- •contain upper and lower case letters

- •are longer – literally, the longer the stronger

- •can be remembered and not written on something that can be easily found

Size Matters

The longer and more complex the password, the better the password. The best way to do this is to take several words that normally do not occur together to build a passphrase that you can easily remember. For example: This year, my favorite sports team has been playing especially poorly -- they're a "dog." Today, the builders started pouring the "foundation" for the house next door. This happens to be during the "summer." And perhaps I like to play "guitar." The passphrase becomes " DogFoundationSummerGuitar." Notice the mixed case, that is, both upper case and lower case letters.

Now let's add some more complexity by adding some characters and substituting, so there are no "dictionary" words. If we use digits 0 - 9 and special characters (shift-numbers), we can do substitution like zero-for-capital-O. Digit 1 for letter "l." @ or 4 for letter "a," either case. And, to make it better, change the rules for substitution. The first time there is a character "a," use "4." The second time, use "@." And so on. Mangling the passphrase this way, we might end up with:

```
g#ounD@t!on$umM3r&ul7ar.
```

If that's too hard, you might split up the words and add numbers and punctuation marks, like this:

```
!Dog#Foundation$Summer&Guitar*.
```

Some people develop a reasonably complex passphrase they use every time they need a password, but to make it unique to that system, website or application, will prepend (add at the beginning) something related to that website. For example, you might want a long password for Facebook. People post all kinds of things to Facebook; they're a bunch of clowns. So:

```
Clowns!Dog#Foundation$Summer&Guitar*.
```

People tell you "don't write your passwords down." Unfortunately, you quickly have more passwords than you can remember. So: get a good encryption program. Choose a decent passphrase for encrypting this collection of files. The passphrase should not be similar to or correlated with your other passwords. Keep an encrypted text file with your user names and passwords. Only open it when you need to remember a password. Keep an encrypted backup of that file somewhere (like a USB drive), so if your disk crashes, you don't lose all your passphrases.

And don't call your password file "Passwords." Give it a different name like "Grocery List" or "urinary tract infection dates." Just don't call it passwords.

Feed Your Head: A Strong Password Is a Long Password

More from Cor:

"A password of two characters from a character set of 26 letters and 10 digits does not have 2^{36} possible combinations, but 36^2. You have 36 choices for the first character and can combine them with 36 choices for the next character. 1296 different passwords are possible.

Similarly a password of eight characters from a character set of 26 letters and 10 digits is not 8^{36}, but 36^8. So roughly 2.820.000.000.000 different passwords are possible."

(Notice how Cor uses the European period Instead of the comma to separate number groups because he's Dutch.)

"Further it is a fallacy to state that passwords must contain certain sub-character sets. This is easiest to see with a two character password from the above set, but with the requirement that it has to contain at least one digit and at least one letter.

For letter+digit there are 26x10=260 different passwords possible and for digit+letter here are 10x26=260 different passwords possible, a total of 520 different passwords. Now compare that to the original 1296 different passwords. Because there are rules about the construction of the passwords, some combinations are invalid. Every invalid combination decreases the size of the **keyspace**.

Strong passwords are long. That's it. They have to be long. This is the main thing. Further, to allow for more complexity, you should allow as many characters in the character set as possible and no restrictions. The restriction reduces the keyspace.

There is an exception for Microsoft Windows with NTLM compatibility (passwords are stored as two hashes for two chunks of seven bytes each). Using a password of 15 characters of more eliminates that risk, because there is no NTLM compatibility for such passwords (max length for NTLM is 14 chars)."

Other Methods

There are many password generators available on the Internet, but these will generate a nearly impossible to remember password.

Try instead to use a seemingly random string of letters or numbers that you can easily recall.

For example:

gandt3b! (goldilocks and the 3 bears!)

JJPL2c1d (john, jill, paul, lucy, 2 cats, 1 dog – the members of your household)

Or you could create your own algorithm to generate passwords. An algorithm is the designation of a step by step procedure for a calculation. Here's an example for you.

This algorithm for choosing a strong password will be the following:

- The last 2 digits of a birth year

- The first 3 letters of a first name, with the last one being in uppercase

- the symbol '!'

- 3 letters to define the service you could registering in

So, that is the algorithm. Let's build a password for Facebook and Gmail, shall we?

A password for Facebook, following this algorithm would be: 84maR!Fac

The password for Gmail, following this algorithm would be: 84maR!Gma

Easy? That way we just created a 9 character password that contains numbers, letters (lowercase and uppercase) and special characters.

This way you have strong passwords and a different one for every service. Of course, everything has a weakness. The password is only as strong as the protection for the algorithm and the length of the characters. If someone discovers your algorithm, it would mean that all your passwords would have been compromised or potentially stolen.

Search online for password managers. You have several free options that you can try out. The password managers are computer applications that you protect with a master password, and can keep all your other passwords in there so you don't have to remember all of them. That way, it's easy to have strong passwords for everything that is important.

Check, Please

So, you think you have the best password ever created. Your password will withstand ten thousand years of attacks because you built it using the rules we've outlined above.

You're a great student of Hacker Highschool, so you applied your knowledge to make an unbreakable password. Before you celebrate, you want to see how well it stands up to a password checker.

Like anything built for quality, you need to test your great creation. How do you do that? You can beat on it with Javascripts that you can trust to apply maximum pressure to your device. Below you will find one of the best password checkers available, and it's free. Go ahead, don't be shy. Hey, why are sweating so much? You look a little nervous.

One key to being a successful security professional is being able to test your own designs. Try and break into your servers or web pages. Locate the weaknesses and correct those vulnerabilities. The same principle applies to passwords. You have to test everything to its limits, no holding back, right? Other attackers aren't going to hold back either so why should you?

Password Strength Checker: There are too many to mention here and they're all free online. Easy to use, too. Many apps now have them built-in and tell you how strong your password is based on some arbitrary rules of the software developer. You don't need them and you don't want them. Think about why.

Exercises

4.25 Explain why you should not use a password checking service for security reasons and why you wouldn't need to anyway.

Change Up

Just like your socks, passwords need to be changed on a regular basis. Please change your password a little more often than you change your socks though. Besides that, passwords are a whole lot easier to change than it is to locate a clean and matching pair of socks. Look under the bed and you will find that other sock. Trust us. Move the cobwebs out of the way and those old books, you'll find that one sock next to the dirty sandwich plate under your bed.

The rule of thumb for updating a password is to "create a new password based on the sensitivity of the access." Yes, this is a lousy rule of thumb but you should apply password updating like this:

- Financial Institutions - Every thirty (30) days

- Medical Records - Update every forty-five (45) days to ninety (90) days

- Government Compartmental (Top Secret and above) - Mandatory every one half hour (ha, ha), really just every hour

- Corporate America - Depends on their own policies; update passwords at least every one hundred and twenty (120) days

- Academic Institutions - Every new semester

- Small Businesses - Change all passwords at least every one hundred and twenty (120) days

- Not for Profits - Change all passwords at least every one hundred and twenty (120) days or immediately after any visit from Bill Gates. Trust us on this one, how do you think Uncle Gates got his start?

Note: Passwords and accounts for ex-employees should be removed (revoked) on the same working day as their departure from the organization. This doesn't always happen. If you were a contract penetration tester, this would be one of your prime opportunities!

Exercises

4.26 Create a strong password, **that you could remember**, and that scores well at the following web page: www.passwordmeter.com But don't use an actual password you use anywhere!

4.27 Look at the Web pages for three different banks and find out what type of password is needed to allow an account holder to access restricted information. Do the banks also offer recommendations that would lead users to create strong passwords?

4.28 Create your own algorithm for passwords. Go to www.passwordmeter.com. again How do you score?

Understanding Windows Passwords

When it comes to passwords (and many other things, as you're going to learn), Windows is a strange beast. Older Windows versions used **LM Password Hashes** all the way up until

Windows 2000, and later versions up to Windows XP still use it. Windows Vista and later disable this scheme, and it's a good thing for several reasons.

One good question is, where are the password hashes stored? In **SAM files**, in:

```
C:/Windows/System32/Config/
```

This folder is locked to all accounts, even if you are an administrator. You can get into it only by booting to a bootable CD or other OS.

When an LM hash is created, it follows a six-step process:

1. The user's password can't be longer than 14 characters. It's converted into all upper-case letters. This is a problem, because it reduces the keyspace by half, and makes using both upper-case and lower-case letters in passwords useless.

2. The password has null characters added to it, if needed, until it is 14 characters long. This is another problem, because all passwords are the same length, and most of them have the same null characters at the end.

3. The new password is split into two 7-character values.

4. These values are used to create two DES encryption keys, one from each half, with a null bit appended after every seven bits, to create two 64-bit keys. Here's another problem, because DES is really, really weak.

5. Each DES key is used to encrypt a preset ASCII string (KGS!@#$%), resulting in two 8-byte ciphertext values.

6. The two 8-byte ciphertext values are combined to form a 16-byte value, which is the completed LM hash.

Though this sounds complicated, as a hashing scheme it has the structural strength of warm butter. Lots of older systems still use it for backward compatibility, but shouldn't, for one big reason. If a system uses both old LM hashes and newer NTLM hashes, the password is stored in both forms, which lets password crackers conveniently crack the easier format. Sweet!

NTLM is a much newer protocol for Windows authentication. NTLM hashes use MD4 hashing. Here's a unique idea: when you do network authentication the hashed NTLM string is passed along rather than the original plaintext password. In other words, you don't actually need a user's password; you just need the hashed version, which you can capture over the network. Bad idea, really bad.

A typical NTLM hash is case sensitive, has an unlimited length and is a stronger networking hashing algorithm than its counterpart LM network hash. NTLM is the protocol used specifically for password hashing whereas NTLM-AUTH is used for network-based remote authentication requests when interacting with services. There are various different flavours of NTLM, such as NTLM-AUTH, NTLM-V1, NTLM-V2, NTLM2, and flavors can vary based on whether they are signed or not.

NTLM Operations

NTLM authenticates with remote services through a **handshake** that consists of three messages being sent, known as type1, type2, and type3.

Typical type1 message (handshake initiation/NTLMSSP_NEGOTIATE):

```
NTLMSSP identifier: NTLMSSP
NTLM Message Type: NTLMSSP_NEGOTIATE (0x00000001)
Flags: 0x00088207
Calling workstation domain: NULL
Calling workstation name: NULL
```

What's happening here is that the client is interacting with the server, initiating a handshake listing which flags it supports, and the name of the workstation and the domain it belongs to.

Typical type2 message (Sever Response/NTLMSSP_CHALLENGE):

```
NTLMSSP identifier: NTLMSSP
NTLM Message Type: NTLMSSP_CHALLENGE (0x00000002)
Domain: DOMAIN
Flags: 0x62818215
NTLM Challenge: 1122334455667788
Reserved: 0000000000000000
Address List
Length: 102
Maxlen: 102
Offset: 68
Domain NetBIOS Name: DOMAIN
Server NetBIOS Name: HOSTNAME
Domain DNS Name: DOMAIN.TLD
Server DNS Name: SEVER.DOMAIN.TLD
List Terminator
```

In a type1 message the server does not yet know who the person initiating the handshake is because no user name information has been sent, only domain info which is not of much use.

In the type2 message, the server responds with its supported flags and domain information. It also responds with the NTLM Challenge string. This string has a unique dynamic value and it is used to salt the password hash to add an extra layer of security. The client then authenticates and completes the handshake with a type3 message.

Typical type3 message (final auth/NTLMSSP_AUTH):

```
NTLMSSP identifier: NTLMSSP
NTLM Message Type: NTLMSSP_AUTH (0x00000003)
Lan Manager Response: 74795D4390C7DDEFB7DAD5D4373066CBF05D633F47F4F12B
NTLM Response: 74795D4390C7DDEFB7DAD5D4374066CBF05D633F47F4F12B
Domain name: DOMAIN
User name: USERNAME
Host name: HOSTNAME
Session Key: Empty
Flags: 0x00008205
```

The NTLM response is generated by the server challenge being hashed with the password challenge. The user name and workstation name for the domain it belongs to are also sent, as well as a session key, if session signing is supported.

The examples above are typical for NTLM-1. NTLM-2 is different because it uses a client challenge as mitigation against attempted rainbow table attacks. NTLM-2 also has additional parameters added into the password response.

Integrated Windows Authentication

Integrated Windows Authentication is an even weirder animal, working mostly through Internet Explorer for local domain authentication. IWA makes it unnecessary for a user to re-enter their password every time they to different services. For example, when you connect to a domain you are connecting to a network share and other services, but Windows won't ask you to re-enter your password for each individual service. Instead it just queries IWA to automatically authenticate. **Trusted site zones** confine this inside a single domain. IWA does a DNS query of the domain name and the DNS hostname, then sends a broadcast request across the local network for the domain authentication.

Pass The Hash

Pass The Hash is a well-known attack vector that exploits NTLM by allowing the attacker to successfully authenticate to a remote service without needing the plaintext password, instead using the NTLM hash. This bypasses the need to crack the NTLM hashes in order to get the password, as it allows practically the same level of access without even bothering. Usually an attacker grabs these authentication hashes from local storage within volatile memory (RAM), for example in a **cold-boot attack**). The problem with this attack method is that it generally requires local admin access on the system.

NTLM Relaying Methods

NTLM Relaying is a less-known attack method that doesn't require you to get admin access in advance, but instead can be performed from a guest account as long as a connection can be made to the network being attacked.

Here's how it works: when you authenticate to a server, shouldn't the server also authenticate itself to you? But in NTLM (and most systems) this doesn't happen. So a fake server can "authenticate" you, then you can use your NTLM hash to "authenticate" to other systems.

NTLM Relaying works by setting up a rogue server which takes in the authentication requests and relays them to another target server. In 2008 Microsoft patched the vulnerability in which an attacker bounces an NTLM request back to themselves (via SMB or even Telnet through the use of the **IE telnet:// exploit**), but due to the design of the protocol, they could still be bounced to other hosts. There are lots of different protocols NTLM can be relayed to, besides the obvious SMB and HTTP; other protocols include MSSQL, LDAP, RDP, PPTP, and many more.

In order to exploit NTLM this way, an HTTP and SMB rogue server needs to be set up on a remote connection. The rogue server needs to keep the user authenticating as much as possible (rather than disconnecting after a single authentication). On a Windows LAN using SMB you can make it authenticate around 30 times total before terminating the connection. To make this work we need to know who the user is in order to keep them authenticating (something which generally isn't known until the type3 handshake response). This can be tricky to do, because within SMB the source IP and port isn't enough information if the attack is being performed externally, while HTTP, WPAD and similar protocols don't always support cookies. The rogue HTTP server should use a HTTP-302 Redirect with Keep-Alive in order to keep the socket open, preventing the session from closing, meaning that once the authentication is complete, we know who the target user is for the rest of that session while the connection remains open.

To make sure authentication happens with the rogue SMB server before bouncing the attacker to other services, some payloads need to be added. WPAD implementation is a must as it will check DNS and then check broadcasting to the network. By default Windows will automatically authenticate to the WPAD sever over HTTP using the currently logged-in user's credentials, which then can be spoofed and reused (although there are limitations, since you usually would have to be internal to the network or would have to spoof NBNS or DNS).

Social engineering comes into play when an attacker puts a UNC network path inside image tags, for example, and the browser automatically connects back to Windows, authenticates with the network share and attempts to grab the image or JavaScript or iframe or whatever goodie. Once the victim downloads this payload, bingo: they're pwned. Some browsers attempt to mitigate this by checking to see whether the network share is within the file security context. This can easily be bypassed by setting headers for a forced download, which is then opened from the download location resulting in access to the file security context which will lead to automatic authentication to the SMB share which will then authenticate to the rogue server. Whew.

There are still problems with this method because it relies on the victim downloading something. Common browser plugins are the solution, because they can establish authentication to the rogue server via SMB. iTunes and Quicktime are easy targets because you can create a playlist with a UNC network path that will automatically authenticate and bypass the local security context.

Another method that can be used for automatic authentication to the rogue server involves vulnerable email clients. For example, if an HTML email that contains a network share is read using Outlook then it will automatically authenticate. Or an attacker can create **desktop.ini** files that say that the icon resource or wallpaper for that folder is a network share, resulting in automatic authentication with the credentials. This method also works with **.lnk** files.

Yet another method: traditional man-in-the-middle attacks to redirect NTLM-AUTH requests, or to inject content into web pages viewed by the victim.

Samdump

Syskey is a Windows utility that encrypts the hashed password information in a SAM database using a 128-bit RC4 encryption key. By default, the SYSKEY encryption key is held in a hidden area in the Windows registry, but it can also be configured to require a password by the user at startup or from an external storage device like a USB drive.

Syskey came as an optional feature in Windows NT 4.0 SP3. It was supposed to protect against offline password cracking attacks, because if you don't have the syskey you can't decrypt the SAM database. Unfortunately these days it's misused by phone scammers and online criminals to lock the computers of naïve victims.

Samdump will extract the syskey password stored locally from the registry to decrypt the SAM database.

The extracted hash can also used for offline cracking, or paid websites can (sometimes) crack the passwords, for instance http://www.onlinehashcrack.com/multi-hash-cracking.php.

Other Password Hashes from Dumps

A popular one is fgdump. Run it from the command line as an administrator to dump the local machine password:

```
fgdump -v
```

Dump a remote machine password:

```
fgdump -v -h hostname -u username -p password
```

You'll need the username and password for a domain administrator account.

Copy the output, which will be a .pwdump file, and use any hash cracking tool to crack the hash.

Similar utilities to extract password hashes from dumps are:

pwdump - http://foofus.net/goons/fizzgig/pwdump/

creddump - http://code.google.com/p/creddump/downloads/list

gsecdump - http://www.truesec.se/sakerhet/verktyg/saakerhet/

Cain & Abel

One of the top password recovery tools for Windows, Cain & Able is at http://www.oxid.it/. This Windows-only password recovery tool handles a giant variety of tasks. It can recover passwords by sniffing the network, cracking encrypted passwords using dictionary, brute force and cryptanalysis assaults, recording VoIP conversations, decoding scrambled passwords, revealing password boxes, uncovering cached passwords and analysing routing protocols.

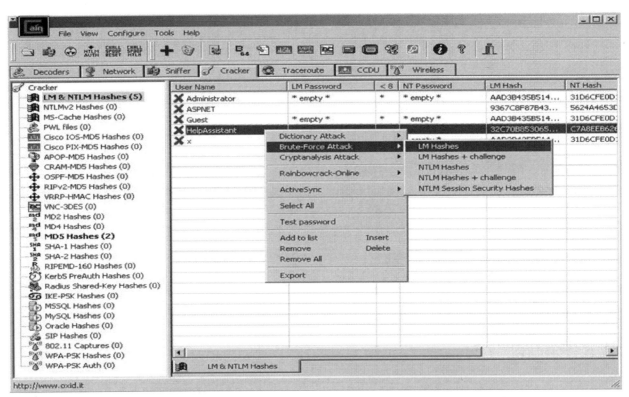

Figure 4.7: Remote NT Hash Dumper in Cain & Abel

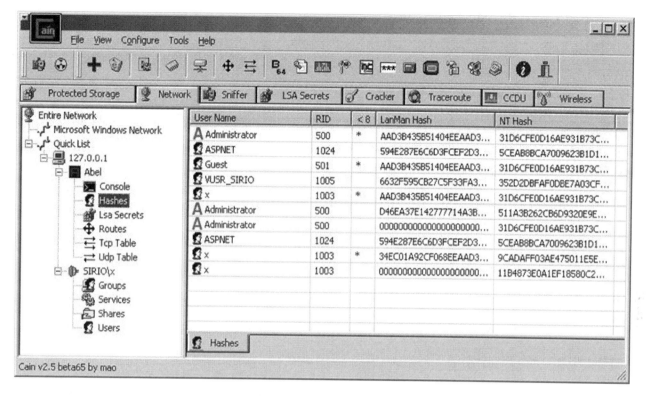

Figure 4.8: Password cracker in Cain & Abel

Conclusion to Hacking Passwords

Have you figured out why NOT to use free online password checkers?
Because you GIVE YOUR PASSWORD AWAY to them!

It has always been difficult to bridge privacy and confidentiality with ease of use for any form of communication. Remember that the Internet was never designed with security in mind. The Internet was design for freedom of information flow to be its primary purpose, even in the event of a failure within the network. Fail-safes were built in to ensure data continued to reach its destination even in the event of a nuclear war. This massive network was built back in a time of flowers and peace signs everywhere but the Soviet Union and United States posed a serious threat to the world. It was called "Mutually Assured Destruction" or MAD because of the nuclear arsenal both countries possessed. But that is another story for another time.

Passwords were introduced when people wanted some sort or privacy on their digital communications. It was an easy and inexpensive band-aid to apply in Unix environments. The young Internet was built to connect university academics, researchers and DoD agencies who funded that research. A username and password allowed a certain amount of security to this fundamental network.

Over time, other commercial organizations and private entities plugged into the Internet, thus expanding the capabilities of this data sharing network. Each company wanted to keep their data separate from prying eyes so passwords were also introduced because they were already part of the Internet culture.

As far back as the 1960's academics and researchers brought up the vulnerabilities of passwords and many advocated for stronger authentication measures. Passwords were inexpensive and easy to use. Year after year password use never faded as it was supposed to. Most security experts fully expected passwords to be replaced with a stronger method. As you can see, that still hasn't happened. The culture of insecure practices continues because it's easier than fixing the problem.

Some powerful organizations have spent millions trying to devise ways to replace passwords with other systems. IBM created a database of personal questions that could be asked before access would be granted. Microsoft worked on using pictures that the user would recognize to gain account privileges. One company came out with voice recognition that was easily tricked using phone conversation recordings. Biometrics has been the Holy Grail of password replacement even though each attempt has been hacked using simple techniques.

In this lesson we showed you lots of information about passwords and how they work (or don't work). Words like "entropy" might not mean much to you at the moment but you will heard it again in your career as a security professional. Hacker Highschool is all about getting you prepared for the real world of cyber security the ISECOM way. You were shown the inner workings of CAPTCA and how it can be bypassed. Multifactor authentication is another large word thrown around by security vendors to sound cool but it just means there are a couple of different ways to prove trust.

Hacker Highschool expects you to be asking questions about the world around you. We demand that you poke around and tinker with things. Questions you should be asking when it comes to passwords include:

- How are passwords stored?

- Where are they stored?

- Are they transmitted or is just the hash transmitted?

- Are default passwords hardcoded into systems?

- Is there a more intelligent method for brute force password attacks?

- Do passwords reset when a system is upgraded or updated?

Be curious about how things have always been operating. Don't expect a book or the Internet to have all the answers. Sometimes you'll have to learn the hard way, by making a mistake. That is okay, though. Experience is gained through mistakes.

Throughout this lesson you were peppered with lots of **Feed Your Head** segments. This was done to highlight some of the highly technical (or really stupid) aspects of passwords. Either way, you should have learned something new. We also discussed biometrics, attacks, hacks, habits, key functions, rainbows, wifi cracking, key sizes, hashes and all kinds of other words not usually found together.

Depending on how passwords are implemented, they can either be complex or rudimentary. It is your job to make systems more secure but not more difficult for the user. This isn't an easy task but one we know you are ready for.

Alphabetical Index

NO WORRIES!
OSSTMMTRAINING.ORG

KNOWING HOW TO APPLY THE OSSTMM TAKES YOUR WORRIES AWAY.
OSSTMM TRAINING MAKES YOU A BETTER, MORE EFFICIENT SECURITY TESTER
AND ANALYST WHICH MAKES WHAT YOU NEED TO SECURE BE MORE SECURE.

ISECOM

Made in the USA
Las Vegas, NV
25 November 2024

12593967R00136